Amend-able?	Motions to Which It Applies	Motions Applied to ...	
No	None	None	Majority
Yes[b]	None	Amend[b]	Majority
No	Main	None	Majority
No	Debatable	None	2/3
Yes[b]	Debatable	Amend[b]	2/3
Yes[b]	Main	Amend,[b] vote immediately, limit debate	Majority
Yes[b]	Main	Amend,[b] vote immediately, limit debate	Majority
Yes[b]	Main	Amend,[b] vote immediately, limit debate	Majority
Yes	Rewordable	Vote immediately, limit debate	Majority
Yes	None	Specific main, subsidiary	Majority
No	Main	Vote immediately, limit debate	Majority
No	Main	Vote immediately, limit debate	Majority
No	Main	None	Majority
No	Rulings of chair	Vote immediately, limit debate	Negative majority
No	None	None	2/3
No	Main	None	Majority

RULES

OF

ORDER

RULES

OF

ORDER

James E. Davis, M.D.

Former Speaker
House of Delegates
American Medical Association

Past President
American Medical Association

Chicago Review Press

**Library of Congress
Cataloging-in-Publication Data**

Davis, James E., 1918–
    Rules of order / James E. Davis. — 1st ed.
        p.   cm.
    Includes bibliographical references and index.
    ISBN 1-55652-150-2
    1. American Medical Association—Rules and
practice.   2. Parliamentary practice.   I. Title.
    R15.D285   1992
    610'.6'073—dc20   92-895
                                                            CIP

Published by Chicago Review Press, Incorporated
814 North Franklin Street
Chicago, Illinois 60610

First edition
First printing

Printed in the United States of America

ISBN 1-55652-150-2

Contents

Preface

Parliamentary procedure truly is the guardian of democracy.

Democracy is based on free speech, majority rule, and the ability of people to govern themselves. In support of these underpinnings of democracy there must be rules of procedure that are fair and equitable to all. And to be understood clearly and used extensively, these rules must be based on principles rather than technicalities, reason rather than memory.

Not since the appearance of *Sturgis Standard Code of Parliamentary Procedure* in 1950 has there been a substantive text that addresses the *current* usage of parliamentary procedure, that strives to preserve the essential and disregard the obsolete, and that seeks to present that basic material in the clearest, easiest understood, and most readily applicable manner. The tendency of existing texts is to expand continually, to become encyclopedic. They thus become references for the shelf rather than a working guide for the lectern. The 1990 edition of *Robert's Rules of Order* contains more than seven hundred pages.

This effort does not represent merely the opinions of an individual or of a group of parliamentarians, for many have been consulted, but it describes the practices of many of the most authoritative deliberative bodies in the country. We approach parliamentary procedure from the position of the presiding officer working with assembly members as they together *practice* parliamentary procedure, as they enjoy it and derive satisfaction from their accomplishments. To make this work authoritative yet not entangled in legal dogma, reliable yet not laborious, has been our goal.

Readers and users of this text—and it is constructed to be used conveniently and constantly—will note significant changes from previous parliamentary works. We have studied carefully every parliamentary action and, freed from the shackles of custom, tradition, and bias, have categorized each according to its function and usage. We have retained as motions only those actions which are necessary for an assembly to accomplish its work. We have emphasized the motions with precedence and their ranking since they are most frequently needed, and we have separated incidental motions from them.

Some actions previously known as motions are in fact requests and are most efficiently handled as such. Some requests are automatic (point of order, parliamentary inquiry, and division of assembly) in that they *must* be granted by the presiding officer. We call these *mandatory requests.* Other requests may be refused by the chair or objected to by the assembly, in either case resulting in a vote. Question of privilege (formerly treated as a motion), withdraw motion, and division of question are examples of these *conditional requests.*

These clarifications render the group of precedented ("workhorse") motions small and easily comprehended. Those experienced in parliamentary usage will readily recall them; the inexperienced will easily find them in Table 1, which appears both on pages 20–21 of the text and on the front endpapers.

We have added the motion to refer for decision, as distinguished from the motion to refer for report, and assigned it a ranking just above the motion to refer. If the assembly chooses to grant its decision-making authority to another body, such as a board of trustees, on a specific item, it may do so. The matter may require study but the need for decision (and possible action) may be urgent and may be required before the assembly will meet again.

Modern parliamentary usage has progressed from moving the previous question or shouting "Question!" to the motion to terminate debate and vote immediately. Rather than use that motion or even the motion to terminate debate, we prefer the motion to vote immediately as it is more dynamic, more definitive, and more easily understood.

The recommendation by some that a two-thirds vote be required when the motion to postpone temporarily (table) is used to set aside the motion or to kill it without debate is unworkable. It often will be impossible to accurately gauge the intent of the proposer of such a motion. A majority vote is proper for this motion.

Current lifestyles revolve around meetings; we are all frequently involved in meetings in our work, schools, churches, organizations, and social groups. Conventions of all types are held constantly. Happily, many areas of the world are now having democratic meetings for the first time or for the first time in decades. For these reasons, the chapters on meetings and conventions should prove especially helpful.

Because we have striven to limit the content of this work to that which is useful and usable daily, material peripheral to practical parliamentary procedure has been treated in less detail. This information will be found in the Appendices.

Throughout the text we have shown that in small meetings the rules can be applied more informally than in a meeting of five hundred individuals, where firm control is essential. However, when a vote is taken, it must be done properly and legally.

If the users of this text find their work in parliamentary procedure easier, more enjoyable, and more satisfying, our purpose will have been served.

Parliamentary Procedure and Its Usage

Our Heritage

Humans learned the ways and the value of orderly, deliberative action in tribal counsels, community gatherings, and war parleys long before we learned to read history. The Bible describes the Council of Seventy chosen to assist Moses, and as early as 1200 B.C. there were references to deliberative assemblies in the Hebrew Commonwealth.

GREEK AND ROMAN

In Athens the assembly (*ecclesia*) met regularly to listen to political and military leaders and to take action. By the age of Pericles (500 B.C.) the meetings were well organized, well attended, and conducted in an orderly fashion. The assembly, presided over by the chairman, worked from a prepared agenda, listened to all who wished to speak, and passed motions or propositions before it. Even motions to limit or to prevent debate were handled fairly. Voting was usually by a show of hands, and the body was bound by the will of the majority. The Roman Senate, the highest of many deliberative authorities, observed great formality in its actions, customs, traditions, and dress. Draco was so strict that his harshness is preserved in our word *draconian*.

BRITISH

Under the British feudal system each baron was required to advise the king on any matter on which he might request the baron's opinion. Great Councils were feudal assemblies summoned by the king to give him such advice. The word *parliament* was used to describe any important meeting held for the purpose of discussion. As early as 1258 the nature of parliaments changed: the barons were invited not only to express opinions for the king but to discuss with each other all pertinent issues, rather than just "the king's business." During the sixteenth century the journal of the House of Commons became established as a source of precedent on matters of procedure. The journal was given official status as a document of the House of Commons in 1623. A compilation of the rulings of Parliament was published by John Hatsell, clerk of the House of Commons, in 1781. This was referred to as Hatsell's *Precedence* and became the authority for parliamentary law.

AMERICAN

Our American system was an adaptation of the already well developed system of the British Parliament. Because the early colonies were widely separated, at times isolated, from one another, local variations developed and were perpetuated. Thomas Jefferson, while serving as vice president of the United States and president of the Senate, recognized the need to record and have both houses of Congress adopt a single set of procedures. His *Manual of Parliamentary Practice,* published in 1801, was derived from the principal English source, Hatsell's *Precedence of Proceedings in the House of Commons,* combined with local traditions. Jefferson was primarily seeking a manual which would incorporate precedence of various legislative bodies. His work was adopted by the Senate, for a time by the House of Representatives, by state legislatures, and by various official bodies.

Subsequently, as society in the New World became more sophisticated, various types of voluntary political, cultural, scientific, charitable, and religious societies evolved. These organizations acutely increased the need for a body of rules adapted to the requirements of nonlegislative organizations. Luther Stearns Cushing, a Massachusetts lawyer and judge, in 1845 published his *Manual of Parliamentary Practice: Rules of Proceedings and Debate in Deliberative Assemblies.* It filled a vast need and was extensively used, emphasizing principles rather than rules and being adapted to the needs of deliberative bodies of the time.

In the latter half of the nineteenth century, Henry Martyn Robert, an engineering officer in the regular army, was active in church, civic, and educational work in the many areas of the country in which he was stationed. He found local parliamentary traditions and customs, while varying among communities, to be firmly entrenched and vigorously defended in each. Those who moved from one area to another found that "friction as to what constituted parliamentary law was indeed not uncommon!"[1] Henry Robert recognized the need for a new kind of parliamentary manual based in its general principles on the rules and practice of Congress and adapted in its details to the use of ordinary societies. He anticipated that various organizations throughout the country would voluntarily adopt such a manual as their official parliamentary reference, thereby establishing a national authority. In spite of the fact that his book emphasized technicalities rather than principles, his success far exceeded his expectations and his *Robert's Rules of Order,* first published on 19 February 1876, became the standard parliamentary source for organizations of all types. His work has undergone several revisions in an effort to keep it current.

In more recent years, many authors have written extensively on parliamentary subjects and many have helped to clarify and simplify the basic body of knowledge. Of special note was the publication by Alice Sturgis in 1950 of an outstanding work which has become known as the *Sturgis Standard Code of Parliamentary Procedure.*[2] In a very clear fashion and few pages, Sturgis outlined the basic rules of deliberative conduct, making a lasting contribution to the subject. Her text truly emphasizes principles rather than technicalities and uses clearer, more easily understood language than does Robert's. Because of the accuracy, clarity, and simplicity of Sturgis's work, it has been adopted as the authority by many organizations in lieu of *Robert's Rules of Order.* An expanded, bulkier revision of Sturgis's work has recently been published by a revision committee of the American Institute of Parliamentarians.[3]

Purpose of Parliamentary Procedure

The purpose of parliamentary procedure has been defined variously by those who studied it most.

Jefferson: "To attain accuracy in business, economy of time, order, uniformity and impartiality."[4]

Cushing: "To subserve the will of the assembly rather than to restrain it; to facilitate, and not to obstruct its deliberate sense."[5]

Robert: "To enable an assembly, with the least possible friction, to deliberate upon questions in which it is interested, and to ascertain and express its deliberate sense or will on these questions."[6]

DeMeter: "To transact the assembly's business legally and to control the conduct of its members."[7]

Sturgis: "To facilitate the transaction of business and to promote cooperation and harmony."[8]

Obviously, each of these authors is correct in his or her individual concept of parliamentary procedure.

Parliamentary procedure is not the stilted, ritualized system that allows those who know it best to take advantage of their less knowledgeable colleagues. To the contrary, parliamentary procedure is the great leveler that assures protection and equal access to all members. It guarantees that the playing field remains level for all.

Truly, parliamentary procedure is the guardian of democracy. Countries, communities, societies, and organizations which allow and promote free speech must have parliamentary procedure; they must have it to guarantee free speech. Nondemocratic groups fear parliamentary procedure; they do not allow it.

If we are to have what Thomas Jefferson called "equal and exact justice to all men" not only must all people have the right of free and fair debate, the right of the majority to decide, and the right of the minority to protest and be protected, but free people must exercise that right. To do so properly they must have a procedure that is understood by all, agreed to by all, and followed by all. Parliamentary law is that procedure. It is simply the mechanism whereby democratic principles are protected.

When Must Parliamentary Procedure Be Used?

Technically, all groups except governments must follow parliamentary procedure when they meet to conduct their business. Governmental bodies—state, national, or international—develop special detailed sets of rules, adopted by their members, which meet their particular needs. Consequently, they do not follow parliamentary procedure as we know it and would find it inadequate were they to try. All other groups, regardless of their type of organization, their mission, or the extent of their knowledge and expertise, must follow parliamentary procedure. Almost every detail of this established procedure has in time been ruled upon by our courts; and thus parliamentary procedure has become a portion of our common law.

There are occasions, especially when a meeting has been convened for purely educational purposes or for the dissemination of information, on which almost no rules or procedures are required. However, when the group is considering action items, in which proposals will be made and discussed and decisions reached, strict adherence to parliamentary rules is required. These decisions are not legal if such procedures have not been followed. Ours is a society which has become accustomed to many and frequent meetings; yet even in small formal groups, members expect that everyone will have an opportunity to speak and vote, that the will of the majority will prevail, and that proper procedure will be followed. The proper use of parliamentary rules ensures this. It also ensures that while the rights of the minority will be protected, a tyranny of the minority will never occur.

When Is Parliamentary Procedure Overruled?

Every organization has the right to make its own rules and to adopt a parliamentary authority which it will follow in its deliberations. However, to be valid the rules adopted must be consonant with the authority of three overruling documents. In ascending order of authority, these are the following:

1. The organization's own constitution and/or bylaws or those of a parent organization.
2. The charter granted by a parent organization to a constituent unit. This charter outranks the subsidiary organization's constitution and bylaws, which must be consonant with the char-

ter. If the organization is incorporated, the charter granted it by government outranks its organizational charter, constitution, and by-laws. All the latter must be consonant with the governmental charter.

3. The laws of federal, state, and local governments. These supersede in authority all charters, constitutions, bylaws, and rules and regulations.

In summary, the rules of one source of authority can never conflict with the rules of the sources that rank above it. Though organizations have the right and often the need to adopt rules that change, extend, or overrule standard provisions of parliamentary procedure, none of these adopted rules can interfere with provisions of its own bylaws or charter. Neither can they be contrary to the law. Americans love and expect freedom. Yet no one resents being required to maintain order and to follow specific rules, for it is evident that these provide the mechanism which allows us, through our innumerable organizations and activities, to accomplish what we need and want to do.

Basic Principles of Parliamentary Procedure

Parliamentary procedures are based on principles, few in number, from which rules are derived. An understanding of the fundamental principles allows one to reason out the rules as logical, sometimes obvious, ways of implementing the principles. Consequently, the proper use of parliamentary procedure depends much more on applying reason than on having an excellent memory or ability to recall.

The actions, indeed the very atmosphere, of a properly conducted assembly are based on a sense of fairness and mutual faith among the members. Though differences may become acute, laced by strong emotion and desire, equality for all must be preserved. Success in such settings comes from the legitimate use of parliamentary principles in a persuasive manner, utilizing proper timing, choice of language, choice of supporting speakers, and ability to focus on the important elements of the issue. Success should never be sought by misrepresentation, inadequate representation of the facts, deceit, intimidation, or unrealistic promises. Any temporary success thus procured is apt to be resented by many members, become counterproductive, and even be declared illegal.

BASIC PRINCIPLES OF PARLIAMENTARY PROCEDURE

1. The parliamentary process must be fair, equitable, understood, and consistent.
2. There must be equality among members.
3. Full discussion must be assured.
4. The right to information must be guaranteed.
5. Established order (or precedence) must be followed.
6. Majority opinion must decide.
7. Minority rights must be protected.
8. The simplest and most direct procedure should be used.

FAIR PROCESS

Parliamentary procedure exists to allow and help groups to conduct their business and accomplish their aims by working together cooperatively and harmoniously to resolve their differences—to reach a consensus. It is always constructive and should never be allowed to confuse the issue or attempt to place any member at a disadvantage. Questions from the floor regarding procedure or parliamentary inquiry are encouraged by the presiding officer, never resented or felt to be threatening.

All members have equal rights, privileges, and responsibilities. There are no classes of membership. This conceptual stricture includes the rights to be notified of the meeting, to attend, to speak, to propose motions, to inquire, to persuade, to nominate and be nominated, and to vote.

EQUALITY OF MEMBERS

The presiding officer has a special responsibility to remain impartial and to treat all members equally while assisting the assembly to arrive at its decision. Members also have equal responsibilities, not only to protect their own rights but to preserve the rights of every member and to see that the meeting is conducted in an orderly, fair, and equitable manner. Even though a member may not be engaged in the ongoing debate and has no specific interest or knowledge of the subject being discussed, he or she has the responsibility to question anytime it appears that the rights of a member, and especially a member of what appears to be a minority, might possibly be abridged. It is never presumptuous of an individual member to question the chair if it appears that the proper procedure is not being followed or that fair and equal treatment is not being accorded, for whatever reason.

RIGHT OF DISCUSSION

Every member has an inalienable privilege of expressing his or her opinion freely on each issue as long as he or she acts within the rules. The presiding officer has a special responsibility to provide this opportunity and to protect the speaker from interruption, interference, embarrassment, or harassment. The presiding officer has a similar responsibility to protect the assembly from any speaker who might be tempted to abuse this privilege by speaking too often, too long, or with ill-chosen or abusive language.

Fortunately, most members of an organization understand that the privilege to speak on any and all issues carries an obligation not to abuse the privilege. The wise realize that they are most effective and most persuasive if they speak selectively, infrequently, and courteously.

RIGHT TO INFORMATION ASSURED

Every member has the right, at all times, to procedural information. This includes knowing what question is before the assembly, what stage the debate is in, and what the effect of the issue currently under consideration (amendment, referral, limitation of debate, immediate vote, and so on) will be. Though the member has a responsibility to remain alert, attentive, and informed, he or she should not hesitate to request the help of the presiding officer when it is needed.

The presiding officer must ensure that every member understands the pending motion, must explain any procedural motion if requested to do so, and should be eager to help any member who expresses a desire for help. Not infrequently, a member will be uncertain about how to obtain his or her objective, how best to state a motion, or whether the amendment he or she wants to propose will be in order. No member should hesitate to ask the presiding officer to help; at times another member, when properly recognized, might have a suggestion as to how an end can best be accomplished.

At the time of the vote, the presiding officer must make certain not only that everyone understands the issue but also what an affirmative or negative vote will mean. For example, when a negative vote is recommended (such as by a reference committee) the presiding officer should explain that though the vote will be taken in the affirmative, any member desiring to follow the recommendation should vote in the negative.

ORDER OF PRECEDENCE

Motions with precedence, because of their importance, are assigned a specific priority in relation to all other motions, and this assigned order must be followed. Nonprecedented (incidental) motions have no ranking order; they become in order when the appropriate situation develops, and they must be decided immediately.

Every major work on parliamentary procedure establishes an order of precedence for motions with precedence. An organization, in officially adopting any work as its authority, adopts that work's order of precedence for its own use.

MAJORITY DECIDES

The majority vote decides an issue. The final authority of every organization is the will of a majority of its members. The function of every meeting is to determine the majority will on the issues before it.

Once determined, the decision of the majority becomes the individual decision of every member regardless of how strongly the individual has opposed the issue or how vigorously he or she has argued against it. In accepting membership in an organization, everyone agrees to accept and to be governed by the vote of the majority. A unanimous vote may be impressive in that all members were of the same persuasion, but it is no more binding than the vote of a simple majority. Just as issues are decided by a majority, election and selection processes are determined by a majority vote.

MINORITY PROTECTED

The rights of the minority must be protected. Though the will of the majority ultimately will determine the group's position on every issue, members neither lose the right to oppose it nor lose any privilege, consideration, or respect by doing so. This is true regardless of how unpopular the opposition is, if the opposition is stated in a positive, fair, considerate, and nondemeaning manner, within the rules. Even though the minority position may appear to be represented by only one or two members, all members must help to ensure the right to present it.

MOST DIRECT PROCEDURE USED

Frequently alternative methods can be applied to accomplish a desired purpose. When it becomes evident, from early debate, what the desire of the assembly is, or what specific matters would be voted upon, all members should seek to find the clearest and most direct way to do so. The presiding officer, indeed every member, has a responsibility to suggest an alternative method if it is likely to be better understood, less cumbersome, and more direct and still protects the original intent. For example, motions always should be stated in the affirmative to avoid having to vote yes to not do something or to vote no to do something.

NOTES

1. Robert, H. M., *Robert's Rules of Order* (Glenview: Scott, Foresman, 1876).
2. Sturgis, A. F., *Sturgis Standard Code of Parliamentary Procedure* (New York: McGraw-Hill, 1950).
3. Sturgis, A., *Standard Code of Parliamentary Procedure* (New York: McGraw-Hill, 1988).
4. Jefferson, T., *Jefferson's Manual,* printed with the rules of the Houses of Congress (1781).
5. Cushing, L. S., *Cushing's Manual of Parliamentary Practice* (1907).
6. Robert, H. M., *Robert's Rules of Order* (Glenview: Scott, Foresman, 1876), 20.

7. DeMeter, G., *DeMeter's Manual of Parliamentary Law and Procedure* (Boston: Little, Brown, 1969), 10.

8. Sturgis, A. F., *Learning Parliamentary Procedure* (New York: McGraw-Hill, 1953), 18.

Chapter 2

Motions and Requests

Deliberative bodies accomplish their work through the use of motions and requests.

MOTIONS

A *motion* is a proposal formally made in an assembly or meeting. A motion proposes a specific action or a change in procedure, and the members of an assembly accomplish their work by making decisions on the actions proposed by such motions.

CONDITIONAL REQUESTS

There are two types of requests, conditional and mandatory. A *conditional request* is a request that *may* be granted by the chair. If not granted or if any member objects, the request then becomes a motion and must follow the rules of all motions. The most common types of conditional requests are question of privilege, withdraw motion, and division of the question.

MANDATORY REQUESTS

A *mandatory request* is the expression of a desire of any member of the assembly that a specific procedure be followed. Such a request *must* be granted by the chair. The most frequently used mandatory requests are point of order, parliamentary inquiry, and division of the assembly.

This chapter briefly explains each type of motion and request. Subsequent chapters give details about handling and using each type.

Motions

Motions are subdivided into two categories: motions with precedence and incidental motions.

MOTIONS WITH PRECEDENCE

Motions with precedence are those that have a rank, that is, a relationship or standing relative to all other precedented motions.

There are three types of motions with precedence:

Main motions
Subsidiary motions
Privileged motions

MAIN MOTIONS

Main motions are divided into two groups: general and specific.

A *general main motion* has no specific name and may deal with any appropriate subject which any member wants to introduce. It is usually referred to as the *main motion*.

THE MAIN MOTION

The *main motion* is the foundation upon which all other motions rest. It is shown at the bottom of the pyramid in Table 3 (page 33) since all other motions depend on and relate to it. Its purpose is to bring substantive proposals (as contrasted with procedural matters) forward for consideration, decision, and action. Once a main motion has been proposed by a member and stated by the presiding officer, it becomes the subject for deliberation and decision. It is made when no other business is being considered. Only one main motion can be pending at any one time. Though the most important and most frequently used of all motions, the main motion is lowest in rank; all other motions shown above it in Table 3 rank above it, in ascending order.

SPECIFIC MAIN MOTIONS

Specific main motions have explicit names and do not necessarily follow the same rules as other main motions. The three most common specific main motions are

Reconsider
Rescind
Resume consideration (take from the table)

Examples of less frequently used specific main motions are those to concur, ratify, affirm, reaffirm, and recall.

A specific main motion does not mark the beginning of a particular involvement of the assembly in a substantive manner, as the main motion does. However, like the main motion, a specific main motion can be made only when no other motion is pending.

SUBSIDIARY MOTIONS

Subsidiary motions are so named because they are secondary to other motions, usually the main motion.

If a main motion is pending and it is the sense of the members that the motion should be adopted or not adopted, no further motions are needed. After a full discussion of the matter, a vote will be taken and the issue decided. However, while the main motion is under discussion, some members may want to alter the motion, to have others consider the matter (committee), to postpone further consideration, or in other ways to change the course of discussion. The use of subsidiary motions attached to the main motion allows the members to attempt to accomplish their desired purpose.

Currently, the most frequently used subsidiary motions are

Postpone temporarily (table)
Vote immediately
Limit debate
Postpone definitely
Refer for decision
Refer for report
Amend

PRIVILEGED MOTIONS

Privileged motions need have no relation to the pending main motion but are of such urgency that they are considered immediately. Rather than relating to the subject under discussion, these motions relate to the members and to the assembly. Were it not for their immediacy, they would be main motions and would be considered later.

There are only two privileged motions:

Adjourn
Recess

INCIDENTAL MOTIONS

Incidental motions have no rank or order of precedence but arise incidentally out of the business under consideration. They do not relate directly to the main motion, as subsidiary motions do, but rather to matters of procedure. Consequently, they can be offered at any time the need arises, and they must be decided immediately so that the work of the assembly can continue.

The most frequently used incidental motions are

Appeal
Suspend rules
Consider informally

Requests

There are two types of requests: mandatory and conditional.

MANDATORY REQUESTS

Mandatory requests, sometimes inappropriately called motions, may be made by any member of the presiding officer. These are not debatable, no vote is taken, and they must be granted by the chair.

The most frequently used mandatory requests are

Point of order
Parliamentary inquiry
Division of assembly

CONDITIONAL REQUESTS

Conditional requests are those that the chair is not required to grant and, even if granted, do not stand if there is objection. Under either circumstance a motion is required, it must be voted on, and the issue must be decided immediately.

The most frequently used conditional requests are

Question of privilege
Withdraw motion
Division of question

Potential Changes in Classification of Motions

A secondary motion (subsidiary, privileged, or incidental) is usually classified according to its relation to the main motion. Customarily, a main motion is pending when a secondary motion is proposed. However, certain secondary motions may be proposed when no main motion is under consideration and they then are classified as main motions.

The following types of secondary motions fall in the latter category and may be presented as main motions when no main motion is under consideration. (An example is given of a possible use of each type of motion.)

Subsidiary Motions

Limit debate (applied to action not already begun)

MEMBER: I move that consideration of the budget, which will occur later in the agenda, be limited to two hours.

Postpone definitely

MEMBER: I move that consideration of the budget, scheduled for today, be postponed to become the first item of business tomorrow morning.

Refer for decision

MEMBER: I move that the matter of changing the association's policy on reforming Medicare be referred to the board of trustees for decision.

Refer for report

MEMBER: I move that we create a committee on retirees' benefits, refer to it all matters relating to such benefits, and request a report at the October meeting.

Amend (applied to an action already taken)

MEMBER: I move to amend the motion passed this morning, to enlarge the Membership Committee to ten members, by adding, and to require that three of these members be under forty years of age.

Privileged Motions

Since privileged motions, save for their urgency, would normally be main motions, they may be offered independently as main motions.

Adjourn

MEMBER: I move we adjourn this afternoon at four o'clock so that we may attend the president's reception.

Recess

MEMBER: I move that we recess for thirty minutes.

Appeal

PRESIDING OFFICER: The request of the Texas delegation for recognition this afternoon to discuss specific problems within their state is denied because of the pressure of business.

MEMBER: I appeal from the decision of the chair.

Suspend rules

MEMBER: I move that we suspend the rule prohibiting speeches by guests so that the governor may be invited to address our next session.

Consider informally

MEMBER: Since the upcoming matter on how best to increase our membership is extremely complex, I move that we consider it informally without a motion.

Rules of Motions

The basic rules that apply to motions are logical, frequently are self-evident, and usually can be determined by reason.

As a member considers proposing a motion, the following questions can help him or her decide if the time is appropriate, when and how to propose the motion, and how it will be handled by the assembly.

1. What is the motion's precedence? Will I be in order if I attempt to make the motion now?
2. Can I interrupt the speaker? Must I wait until I can get the floor?
3. Will my motion require a second?
4. Is my motion debatable? If so, I want to be prepared to be the first to discuss it.
5. Can my motion be amended? If so, I must be prepared to defend my position or to change it.
6. To what other motions does my motion apply? Is the motion I want to propose applicable to the motion under discussion?
7. What other motions can be applied to my motion? How can the motion I want to propose be changed by other motions?
8. What vote is required for passage? Am I asking for action which will require more than the usual simple majority?
9. When and how can I change a motion already voted on?

The answers to these questions vary with each motion. Many answers will be found by consulting Table 1 on pages 20–21 and on the front endpapers. They are summarized here under some general rules which should help members determine the right answers in specific situations.

WHAT IS THE MOTION'S PRECEDENCE?

The uppermost question in the mind of the member who desires to make a motion is, Am I in order now, or must I wait? Every motion with precedence has assigned to it an order of rank depending on the urgency of the need of the assembly to use it. Consequently, main motions have the lowest precedence, as they are the basic matter to be considered, subject to many possible changes as determined by the assembly. Thus, when a main motion is under consideration, the motion to amend is in order since it has a higher rank, and every other motion with a higher rank is in order. By being familiar with this order of precedence, or by a rapid reference to Table 1, every member can determine whether or not his or her proposed amendment is in order.

CAN I INTERRUPT THE SPEAKER?

Basically, the speaker who has the floor is protected from interruption, but there are times when interruption is necessary and allowed.

Only two motions allow a proposer to interrupt the speaker. These are the motions to reconsider and to appeal, because they must be proposed and decided within a specific time limit. The motion to reconsider must be made during the same meeting or convention at which the original vote was taken. An appeal must be made before other business intervenes.

Many requests, because of their probable urgency, warrant interrupting the speaker.

All of the *mandatory requests,* such as point of order, parliamentary inquiry, and division of assembly, may interrupt. Point of order or parliamentary inquiry must relate to a possible error by the chair, failure to comply with the rules that directly relate to the issue under consideration, or a request for information which is necessary immediately. One should not interrupt to obtain general information, if such a request could just as well wait until the speaker has concluded.

The *conditional requests* of question of privilege and permission to withdraw the motion also permit the requester to interrupt the speaker. Privilege may relate to the immediate convenience, comfort, or rights of the entire assembly or of a single member and understandably should not be delayed. The request for permission to withdraw a motion must be made by the original proposer before the motion is stated by the presiding officer, if the requester desires to avoid a motion. After the motion is stated by the

Table 1   *Rules Governing Motions*

	Interrupt Speaker?	Second Needed?	Debate Allowed?
Precedented Motions[a]			
Privileged Motions			
10. Adjourn	No	Yes	No
9. Recess	No	Yes	Yes[b]
Subsidiary Motions			
8. Postpone Temporarily (Table)	No	Yes	No
7. Vote Immediately	No	Yes	No
6. Limit Debate	No	Yes	Yes[b]
5. Postpone Definitely	No	Yes	Yes[b]
4. Refer for Decision	No	Yes	Yes[b]
3. Refer for Report	No	Yes	Yes[b]
2. Amend	No	Yes	Yes
Main Motions			
1. a. The Main Motion	No	Yes	Yes
b. Specific Main Motions Reconsider	Yes	Yes	Yes[b]
Rescind	No	Yes	Yes
Resume Consideration (Take from the Table)	No	Yes	No
Incidental Motions[c]			
Appeal	Yes	Yes	Yes
Suspend Rules	No	Yes	No
Consider Informally	No	Yes	No

[a] Precedented motions are indicated from 1 to 10 in increasing order of precedence.

[b] Limited use.

[c] Incidental motions must be decided immediately.

Note: The motion to recall, rarely used, has a precedence of $4+$. It is handled exactly like either motion to refer except that it cannot be amended and it applies only to the motion to refer.

Amend- able?	Motions to Which It Applies	Motions That Can Be Applied to It	Vote Required for Passage
No	None	None	Majority
Yes[b]	None	Amend[b]	Majority
No	Main	None	Majority
No	Debatable	None	2/3
Yes[b]	Debatable	Amend[b]	2/3
Yes[b]	Main	Amend,[b] vote immediately, limit debate	Majority
Yes[b]	Main	Amend,[b] vote immediately, limit debate	Majority
Yes[b]	Main	Amend,[b] vote immediately, limit debate	Majority
Yes	Rewordable	Vote immediately, limit debate	Majority
Yes	None	Specific main, subsidiary	Majority
No	Main	Vote immediately, limit debate	Majority
No	Main	Vote immediately, limit debate	Majority
No	Main	None	Majority
No	Rulings of chair	Vote immediately, limit debate	Negative majority
No	None	None	2/3
No	Main	None	Majority

presiding officer, the matter is the property of the assembly and a motion, or at least a declaration that "without objection . . . it is withdrawn," is required.

WILL MOTION REQUIRE A SECOND?

Motions require a second; requests do not. A second indicates that at least one member other than the proposer wants to have the issue discussed. It does not mean that the seconder necessarily agrees with the motion or is committed to vote for it.

The rule that requests do not require a second includes conditional requests (such as question of privilege, withdraw the motion, or division of question) that become motions because the chair denies them or an objection is made.

Reports from an organized part of the parent body, such as a committee, task force, or commission in which at least two members of the parent body serve, do not require a second, as one is automatically included. For clarification, the chair often comments, "This motion comes with a second."

IS MOTION DEBATABLE?

Motions are divided as to whether they are fully debatable, subject to limited debate only, or not debatable.

The only motions that are fully debatable are main motions, amendments to main motions, and motions to rescind and to appeal. Main motions are debatable because they are the workhorse motions that present substantive matters requiring thorough investigation, consideration, and decision. An amendment is debatable if it involves a debatable motion; it is not debatable if the motion it amends is not debatable. Amendments to the main motion therefore are debatable. The motion to rescind is a main motion that reopens the main motion to debate, and consequently it too is fully debatable. The appeal from a decision of the chair is debatable, and both the presiding officer and the appealing member must have an opportunity to state their reasons for the decision and the appeal.

Motions which allow only limited debate are those to recess, limit debate, postpone definitely, refer for decision, refer for report, and reconsider. On each of these only limited, focused discussion on the pertinent matter(s) is allowed. Debate on the motion to recess is limited to the advisability, the time, and the length of recess. The motion to limit debate can be debated only in terms of the need, the nature, and the time of limitation. The motion to postpone definitely limits debate to the advisability of postponing and to the exact time debate will be resumed. Debate on motions to refer for decision and to refer for report is limited to the advisability of doing so, the body to which referral is made, and any instructions the assembly wants to send with the referral. The motion to reconsider is debatable only as to reasons for reconsidering.

All other motions are not debatable because they concern procedural matters which should not require discussion. Specifically, these are the motions to adjourn, to postpone temporarily, to vote immediately, to resume consideration, to suspend rules, and to consider informally.

CAN THE MOTION BE AMENDED?

Any motion that can be stated in language which makes the motion substantially different can be amended. If the assembly can state the motion in language which more accurately expresses its will, it has the right to do so. The motion to adjourn is quite clear; the assembly must decide to adjourn or not, and this is not amendable.

The main motion and the motion to amend are the only motions freely amendable. Specific main motions, since they apply to the main motion, are not amendable; neither are incidental motions.

The motions to recess, to limit debate, and to postpone definitely are amendable only as to time. The motions to refer for report and refer for decision are limited to specific details and instructions to the body receiving the referral.

WHAT MOTIONS CAN BE APPLIED TO OTHERS?

A motion is applicable to another motion when it will dispose of or change in any way the other motion.

The main motion is basic and independent and applies to no other motion. Specific main motions apply only to the main motion.

Subsidiary motions apply only to main motions; the motions to vote immediately and to limit debate are applicable to any debatable motion. The motion to amend applies to any motion that can be changed significantly by different words. Consequently, it is applicable to the main motion and to the motions to amend, to refer for report, to refer for decision, to recall, to postpone definitely, to limit debate, and to recess.

Privileged motions apply to no other motions as they are concerned with the organization and the membership rather than with specific items of business.

Of the incidental motions, the motion to appeal applies only to rulings of the chair, the motion to consider informally applies only to the main motion, and the motion to suspend rules applies to no others.

Requests, except for question of privilege, apply to motions. When a conditional request results in a motion, permission to withdraw motion applies to all other motions and division of question applies only to the main motion.

Of the mandatory requests, parliamentary inquiry applies to all motions, point of order to any motion in which an error is suspected, and division of assembly to any motion on which there is an indecisive vote.

Specific answers about what motions can be applied to others are most easily found in Table 1 and are summarized here.

RULES GOVERNING APPLYING MOTIONS

1. All debatable motions can have the motions to vote immediately and to limit debate applied to them.
2. All motions that can be reworded to produce a different result can have the motion to amend applied to them.
3. The main motion can have specific main motions and subsidiary motions applied to it.
4. Of the specific main motions, the motion to resume consideration can have none applied while the motions to reconsider and to rescind can have the motions to vote immediately and to limit debate applied to them.
5. Of the privileged motions, only the motion to recess can have applied to it the motion to amend in a limited fashion.

6. Of the subsidiary motions, the motions to postpone temporarily and to vote immediately can have no motions applied.

7. All of the remaining subsidiary motions except the motion to amend can have the motion to amend applied in a limited fashion; all the remaining except the motion to limit debate can have the motions to vote immediately and to limit debate applied.

8. Of the incidental motions, only the motion to appeal can have other motions applied, and the only ones to be applied are the motions to vote immediately and to limit debate.

WHAT VOTE IS REQUIRED FOR PASSAGE?

A majority vote is sufficient for passage of all motions except those which, by their actions, may restrict the rights of a member either by changing the rules or by limiting debate. These restrictive motions require a two-thirds vote, and there are only three: the motions to vote immediately, to limit debate, and to suspend the rules.

WHEN AND HOW CAN A MOTION BE CHANGED?

To renew a motion is to propose again the same, or substantially the same, motion that has been voted on and lost at the same meeting or convention. To renew a lost motion or to reconsider a motion carried or lost is often advisable or necessary. When is it appropriate to do so and how is it done?

Any main motion which has carried can be amended by a new main motion at any meeting or convention.

Any motion lost can be renewed by a new main motion at any meeting or convention.

When an assembly has changed its mind on any main motion, either carried or lost, it can address the same issue again by a motion to reconsider, but only at the same meeting or convention.

If the assembly has changed its mind and wants to repeal any main motion carried at any meeting or convention, it can do so by a motion to rescind.

An assembly may, for many reasons, want to reconsider a main motion that was previously referred to a committee, council, or task force; this reconsid-

Table 2
Changing Main Motions Already Voted On

Motion	May Be Used	Applies to
Amend by new main motion	At any meeting or convention	Any main motion carried
Renew by new main motion	At any meeting or convention	Any main motion lost
Motion to reconsider	Only at same meeting or convention	Any main motion carried or lost
Motion to rescind	At any meeting or convention	Any main motion carried
Motion to recall	At any meeting or convention	Any main motion previously referred to a constituent group (such as a committee)
Repeal or amend by implication	At any meeting or convention	Any main motion previously carried which conflicts with later main motion

eration can be done at any meeting or convention by a motion to recall.

A new motion which is adopted repeals any previous action of the assembly which is in conflict with the new motion. In spite of an extensive search to identify all motions which might be in conflict, a member may feel that inadvertently some previous conflicting action has not been identified. He or she may ensure that all previous conflicts have been corrected by moving that previous conflicting actions be amended or repealed by implication. This may be done at any meeting or convention and applies to any main motion previously carried which conflicts with the current main motion.

These actions are shown in Table 2.

Chapter 4

Presentation and Handling of Motions

The work of an assembly is accomplished by its members making decisions on motions. A meeting may be held for the purpose of deciding a single motion. Larger meetings and conventions will accomplish a heavy workload by deciding hundreds of motions.

PRESENTATION OF MOTION

Any member may propose a motion, which may also be referred to as the question (under discussion), the issue, the proposal, or the proposition.

In smaller, less formal groups, a member usually has no difficulty getting the presiding officer's attention (by raising a finger, hand, or even the eyes). After being recognized verbally by the presiding officer, the member states his or her motion. If the motion is seconded, the member discusses it, as do other members if they so desire, and a vote is taken. Amendments and other subsidiary motions are applicable in any meeting, if they are thought to be helpful or necessary.

In larger meetings, especially in conventions where there may be hundreds of members present and multiple microphones available, the procedure is more complicated. In such a setting, to get his or her idea, plan, or recommendation before the assembly for formal consideration, a member must take several steps correctly and in proper order. The member must do the following:

1. Rise and approach a microphone.
2. Wait until recognized by the presiding officer.
3. Propose his or her motion.
4. Wait until another member seconds the motion.
5. Listen carefully as the presiding officer states the motion to the assembly, to ensure its accuracy.
6. Begin the discussion (if the motion is debatable).

7. Return to his or her seat as the debate continues.

Any member, except the presiding officer, has the right to propose a motion. This may be done at any appropriate time when there is no business before the assembly. The following sections explain in detail the steps in presenting a motion.

ADDRESSING THE PRESIDING OFFICER

To present a motion the member rises and approaches the microphone. When recognized by the presiding officer, the proposer addresses the presiding officer by his or her official title—"Mr. Chair," "Madam Chair," "Mr. President," "Madam Speaker," "Mr. Moderator," and so on. If the presiding officer has no title, or if it is not known to the member, it is always correct to address the presiding officer as "Mr. Chair" or "Madam Chair."

By addressing the presiding officer in this manner, the member indicates that he or she wishes to obtain the floor to make a motion or to speak.

RECOGNITION BY PRESIDING OFFICER

The presiding officer will recognize the members in the order in which they arise or arrive at one of the microphones. In large meetings, the presider keeps a priority list to ensure that he or she recognizes members in the order in which they indicated a desire for recognition. He or she recognizes by calling the member by name, by using a title to differentiate between those standing—as "the delegate from New York"—or by recognizing the microphone being used, as "microphone number one." In conventions using multiple microphones, only the one being used by the person recognized by the chair is activated. The member should be alert and prepared to proceed with his or her statement immediately upon recognition. In large meetings and conventions, members identify themselves and their constituency, regardless of how well they are known, so that everyone is aware of exactly who is speaking and the transcription of the meeting is kept accurate.

PROPOSING THE MOTION

To make a motion, a member begins by saying, "I move that . . ." followed with as clear and succinct a statement of the idea as possible, as "I move that dues for the following year be increased by fifteen dollars." By clearly and unequivocally saying, "I move . . . ," the member alerts the presiding officer and all present that he or she is about to submit a proposal for consideration. No other form should be used. Even though the member, by demeanor and voice, indicates that he or she is about to make a proposal, phrases like "I think . . . ," "I believe . . . ," or "It would be a good thing if . . ." do not introduce a motion and any member who uses them leaves his or her intentions unclear.

After the member makes such a statement, the presiding officer has to inquire of the member as to his or her desire. If it is to make a motion, the presider then restates the motion correctly, as "It has been moved that dues for the following year be increased by fifteen dollars," or asks the member to state it in the proper form.

A brief explanatory remark immediately before or after the motion is permissible, but no discussion is allowed until the motion has been seconded by another member and restated by the presiding officer. If the motion is lengthy or complicated, the proposer should present written copies of it to the presiding officer and secretary. If the meeting is large, and if the motion is longer than one or two sentences, printed copies of the motion should be available and should be passed out to every member.

SECONDING THE MOTION

Any member, without recognition, may second a motion, indicating that he or she wants the assembly to consider the motion. A second does not necessarily indicate an endorsement of the motion.

If there appears not to be a second, the presiding officer states the motion and asks, "Is there a second to the motion?" If there is still not a second, the presiding officer states, "The motion is lost for want of a second."

When a group such as a committee, council, or task force of the larger body is reporting to the parent organization, since at least two members of the appointed group are members of the larger body (and often all members come from the parent group), any recommended action contains a second. Thus, if a committee makes its report and moves for the adoption of the report, the motion is automatically seconded. For the report to have come from the committee with a recommendation, more than one member of the larger body necessarily has agreed to it. If there is confusion or if lack of a second is questioned, the presiding officer simply states, "The motion to adopt this report comes with a second."

STATEMENT OF MOTION BY PRESIDING OFFICER

As soon as the motion has been properly moved and seconded, the presiding officer states the motion to the assembly. He or she states it exactly as did the member presenting the motion unless the presider feels that it has been presented in an unclear and ambiguous fashion. In that case the presider may rephrase the motion without changing its meaning. The proposer has the right to accept or reject the presiding officer's version. If he or she disagrees with the presiding officer, the proposer restates the motion, and that becomes the legal motion.

If the proposed motion would have the assembly do anything that is unlawful or contrary to the constitution and bylaws of the organization, or if it is rude, tasteless, or harmful to the organization, the presiding officer may rule it out of order—as "The chair rules your motion out of order"—providing reasons for the ruling. The proposer or any member may appeal from the ruling of the chair.

Until the presiding officer restates the motion, it is the property of the proposer, who may withdraw or modify it in any way he or she desires. As soon as the presiding officer states the motion to the assembly, the motion is the property of the assembly for its disposition. It is then known as the pending motion, pending question, or pending issue. The assembly must take definitive action on it. However, the decision to take no action, if that is the will of the assembly, is a definitive action.

DISCUSSION

If the motion is debatable, it is customary and courteous for the presiding officer to return to the proposer of the motion to allow him or her to discuss it first. This also serves the assembly well, as it allows the proposer not only to speak on the substance of the motion but to point out, if appropriate, why he or she chose certain words or phrases for the motion. The proposer must follow the same rules that apply to any subsequent speakers if debate is limited in any way by time, rules, and so on. Every member of the assembly is then entitled to discuss the motion, remembering that at all times the discussion should be relevant, courteous, impersonal, and addressed to the chair.

MOVING TO VOTE

As soon as there are no members wishing to discuss the motion further, the presiding officer moves immediately to call for a vote, or alternatively may say, "There appears to be no further discussion," and then, still seeing no member seeking recognition, "We will vote." The presider restates the motion to the assembly, and the vote is taken.

Chapter 5

Motions with Precedence and Their Rank

There are three types of motions with precedence:

Main motions
Subsidiary motions
Privileged motions

Each type of precedented motion includes individual motions, and all motions with precedence are ranked against every other precedented motion. Precedented motions are sometimes called working motions, for their clearly defined order of precedence allows the assembly to be a dynamic body, constantly working toward decision in an orderly, equitable, and understandable manner.

Precedence, which is based on urgency, is established by assigning a definite rank to every motion. The order, or precedence, can be visualized as a pyramid made of layers of blocks with a large, strong base. All layers are dependent on the base, and each layer has a rank according to its position in the pyramid. The higher the layer, the higher the rank (see Table 3 on the next page).

By using this ranking and following two basic rules of precedence, an orderly course can be followed.

RULES OF PRECEDENCE

1. When a motion is being considered, only a motion of higher rank may be proposed.
2. Motions are considered and voted on in reverse order of proposal. The last motion to be proposed is considered first.

These rules might be fixed in the mind by imagining that an assembly has many options in seeking an appropriate course of action. If the solution lies in the main motion as stated, no climbing above the base is necessary. However, the assembly has the option to climb the pyramid (never retreating) until it finds the level which it desires, where it can see the direction to a solution. If, on the motion of any mem-

Table 3
Motions with Precedence and Their Rank

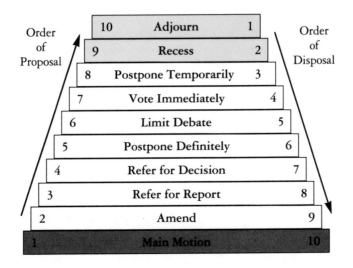

Order of Proposal

Order of Disposal

10	Adjourn	1
9	Recess	2
8	Postpone Temporarily	3
7	Vote Immediately	4
6	Limit Debate	5
5	Postpone Definitely	6
4	Refer for Decision	7
3	Refer for Report	8
2	Amend	9
1	Main Motion	10

Precedented Motions

Privileged Motions

Subsidiary Motions

Main Motion

ber, the assembly believes a more likely view of the solution can be obtained at a higher level, it ascends to that level and all discussion moves to that level. When discussion is completed and voting begins, the assembly must start its descent in an orderly fashion.

EXAMPLE OF PRECEDENCE

The following example shows how precedence operates in a dynamic setting. The numbers in parentheses refer to the levels of precedence represented in Table 3.

A member makes a motion (1) that an assessment of $100 per member be levied, effective 1 January of the next year. After some discussion an amendment (2) to change the amount to $150 per member is made. During the ensuing debate on the amendment it is moved that the entire matter (pending motion and pending amendment) be referred for report (3) to the executive committee. One member stresses the urgency of the matter and the fact that the assembly will not meet until next year to receive the executive committee's report. Therefore, to have the matter studied and the assessment implemented on 1 January, if found feasible, he moves to refer for decision (4) to the executive committee. Still another speaker wants the assembly, rather than the executive committee, to make the decision and consequently moves that consideration of the matter be postponed definitely (5) to the first meeting of the following year. Such a lengthy debate follows that it is moved to limit debate (6) so that every speaker has only two minutes. This motion carries and the next speaker moves to vote immediately (7) on all pending issues. This motion carries.

Consequently, a vote is taken on the highest numbered item of the pending issues, beginning with 5, to postpone definitely. If that motion carries, the issue is postponed to the first meeting of the following year. If the motion fails, then 4, refer for decision, becomes the pending issue and a vote is taken. If this should fail, 3, 2, and 1 are considered in order until affirmative action is taken.

The three types of motions with precedence (main, subsidiary, and privileged) are considered individually in the next chapters.

Chapter 6

Main Motions

Main motions are the most important and most frequently used motions. They are of two types:

The main motion
Specific main motions

The main motion is the basis of all debate, deliberation, and ultimate decision. Specific main motions apply only to the main motion and affect how it is handled. The three most frequently used specific main motions are

Reconsider
Rescind
Resume consideration (take from the table)

The Main Motion

The purpose of the main motion is to bring before the assembly a proposal for discussion and decision. It is the foundation of the pyramid of precedence of motions (see Table 3 on page 33). Since only a single subject can be considered at any one time, the main motion can be proposed only when no other motion is being considered.

INTRODUCING THE MAIN MOTION

Because of its importance and basic nature, the main motion should be well thought out, concise, clear, complete, and unambiguous. If it is not, the presiding officer should restate it (with approval of the proposer) or ask the proposer to rephrase it. The proposer has the ultimate right to approve the wording of the motion.

The main motion should be stated in the affirmative, by the use of the words "I move. . . ." If it is more than a single statement easily comprehended by the assembly, it should be submitted in writing. In a large assembly, a lengthy motion should be printed and a copy circulated to every member. When the motion has been seconded and stated or restated by the presiding officer, the motion becomes the property of the assembly and can be withdrawn only with permission of the assembly.

THE MAIN MOTION AS A RESOLUTION

In formal meetings and conventions, the main motion is often expressed in the form of resolutions, especially when the proposal is long or complex. Such resolutions should be submitted in writing. Most often, the resolved portion is preceded by one or more *whereas*es that state the reasons for the resolves. For example:

> *Whereas,* this association will soon complete its first hundred years of service; and
>
> *Whereas,* this service has been of inestimable value to the American people; and
>
> *Whereas,* the American public should be informed of the accomplishments of this association; therefore be it
>
> *Resolved,* that this association conduct a public information campaign to cost not in excess of $100,000.

The assembly, in adopting a resolution, legally adopts only the resolves. The language of the *whereas*es has no legal status, and, consequently, under most circumstances the assembly should not spend a great deal of time in attempting to come to complete agreement about this language. However, because of the media's intense interest in aspects of the *whereas*es, on occasion it can be important that the assembly take the time and make the effort to ensure that statements made in the *whereas*es are accurate and defensible. Presiding officers should be sensitive to this need and allow the time and opportunity it requires.

DISCUSSING THE MAIN MOTION

When the main motion has been seconded and stated to the assembly by the presiding officer, the motion is open for debate. It cannot be debated before the statement by the presiding officer unless a motion has been passed to consider it informally. It is customary and courteous for the presiding officer to allow the proposer of the motion the first opportunity to explain and discuss the motion.

DISPOSITION OF THE MAIN MOTION

When the presiding officer has stated the motion to the assembly, the assembly is obligated to take definitive action on it.

Another main motion can be substituted for the main motion if it is offered as a substitute amendment to the main motion.

When the main motion has been acted upon and lost, it cannot be renewed (proposed again in the same or essentially the same words) at the same meeting or convention. However, it can be reconsidered at the same meeting or convention.

EFFECT

Adoption of the main motion commits the organization to take the action stated in the motion. If the motion concerns the policy of the organization, then adoption by the assembly changes the policy.

RULES GOVERNING THE MAIN MOTION

1. The speaker cannot be interrupted.
2. The motion requires a second.
3. The motion is debatable.
4. The motion is amendable.
5. The motion applies to no other motion.
6. The motion can have applied to it specific main motions, subsidiary motions, and the request to withdraw.
7. The motion requires a majority vote for passage.
8. The motion takes precedence over no other motion.

Specific Main Motions

The most frequently used specific main motions are

Reconsider
Rescind
Resume consideration (take from the table)

MOTION TO RECONSIDER

The purpose of the motion to reconsider is to allow an assembly to debate and to vote again on a main motion taken at the same meeting or convention, as though no previous vote had been taken on it.

Example

MEMBER: I move to reconsider the motion passed earlier today to appropriate $100,000 for a public information campaign.

PRESIDING OFFICER (after motion is seconded): It has been moved and seconded to reconsider the motion passed earlier today to appropriate $100,000 for a public information campaign. . . . Is there limited discussion on the motion to reconsider? . . . Those in favor of reconsideration, please say Aye. . . . Those opposed to reconsideration, No. . . . The motion to reconsider is carried and the motion to appropriate $100,000 for a public information campaign is again open for discussion.

WHAT MOTIONS CAN BE RECONSIDERED?

Any main motion, whether carried or lost, can be reconsidered at the same meeting or convention. The only exception is when something that cannot be undone has already been effected as a result of the previous vote, for example when funds have been paid, a contract signed, or a time limit has expired.

The motion to reconsider is applied only to the main motion; other motions can be changed in easier and more direct ways. Motions that have been carried can be amended; those that have been lost can be renewed; those that have been referred to a committee can be recalled; those on which action has been postponed temporarily can be reactivated by a motion to resume consideration.

HOW IS IT PROPOSED?

The motion to reconsider may be offered at any time. This motion is unique in that it may interrupt a speaker, it may be proposed though other matters are under consideration, and its proposal suspends any action on the motion that is proposed for reconsideration until the motion to reconsider is decided.

Even though the motion to reconsider may interrupt other business, if it is seconded the presiding officer acknowledges this and announces that he or she will come back to the matter of reconsideration after the pending issue is decided. The presider then returns to the pending business and only after that business is decided does he or she call for a vote on the motion to reconsider. However, if the motion to reconsider is offered when no other business is pending, it is considered immediately.

WHO CAN MOVE TO RECONSIDER?

Any member can offer the motion to reconsider. Historically, the right to move to reconsider was limited only to those who had voted for the original motion, but this is no longer applicable. If the presiding officer considers the motion dilatory (as when it is offered repeatedly) the motion can be ruled out of order. This ruling, like all others, is subject to challenge, ultimately to be decided by the assembly itself.

LIMITED DEBATE

Debate on the motion to reconsider is limited to reasons for reconsidering the motion. Since action on the main motion must await an affirmative vote to reconsider it, the motion to reconsider must be decided immediately.

EFFECT

The motion to reconsider, when adopted, reopens the motion and abolishes the previous vote on the original motion, as though it had never been taken.

RULES GOVERNING THE MOTION TO RECONSIDER

1. The speaker can be interrupted.
2. The motion requires a second.
3. The motion is debatable.
4. The motion is not amendable.
5. The motion applies to the main motion.
6. The motion can have applied to it the motions to vote immediately and to limit debate.
7. The motion requires a majority vote for passage.
8. The motion takes precedence over no other motion.

Motion to Rescind

The purpose of the motion to rescind is to invalidate (repeal) a main motion passed at a previous meeting.

Example
MEMBER: I move to rescind the motion passed at the last meeting to appropriate $100,000 for a

39

public information campaign and to return all unspent funds to the treasury.

PRESIDING OFFICER (after motion is seconded): It has been moved and seconded to rescind the motion passed last month to appropriate $100,000 for a public information campaign and to return all unspent funds to the treasury. . . . Is there discussion? . . . Those in favor of rescinding this action, please say Aye. . . . Those opposed to rescinding, say No. . . . The motion to rescind is carried. The motion that this organization appropriate $100,000 for a public information campaign is rescinded and all unspent funds will be returned to the treasury.

WHAT MOTIONS CAN BE RESCINDED?

Any motion that was carried, regardless of when it was passed, may be rescinded. Obviously, if the full effect of the original motion has been carried out, the motion is moot. However, if only part of the action has been accomplished, as in the preceding example, the remaining action can be rescinded.

The motion to rescind is never retroactive. For example, if the rescinded action affects policy (rather than the payment of funds as in the example), the policy is immediately changed but cannot be applied retroactively.

WHEN CAN IT BE PROPOSED?

The motion to rescind may be offered when no other motion is under consideration.

VOTE REQUIRED

A motion to rescind an action requires the same number of votes as were required to pass it. Most often this is a majority, but if the original motion required a two-thirds majority for passage, a two-thirds majority is required to rescind.

SAME REQUIREMENTS AS ORIGINAL MOTION

If there were special requirements for the original consideration of the motion, such as advance notice to members, written notice to members, and so on, exactly the same manner of handling the motion to rescind is required.

Motion to Rescind and Expunge

Rarely, the motion to expunge is combined with the motion to rescind.

Example

MEMBER: I move to rescind the motion to appropriate $100,000 for a public relations campaign and to expunge this motion from the minutes.

If the motion carries, the previous action is considered not to be part of the minutes. Actually, the secretary does not remove the motion from the minutes but rather highlights it, as by encircling it, marks it "Expunged by order of the assembly" with the date of the action to expunge, and signs it as secretary. The expunged motion is not included in any minutes published in the future but is available as a matter of record.

VOTE REQUIRED

The motion to expunge, since it does not limit the action of the members, requires a majority vote, whether it is used alone or with the motion to rescind.

EFFECT

The motion to expunge, when adopted, repeals (invalidates) the motion from the date and time of the motion to rescind.

RULES GOVERNING THE MOTION TO RESCIND

1. The speaker cannot be interrupted.
2. The motion requires a second.
3. The motion is debatable.
4. The motion is not amendable.
5. The motion applies to the main motion.
6. The motion can have applied to it the motions to vote immediately and to limit debate.
7. The motion requires a majority vote for passage.
8. The motion takes precedence over no other motion.

Motion to Resume Consideration (*Take from the Table*)

The purpose of the motion to resume consideration is to allow an assembly to consider (take from the table) a motion that was postponed temporarily (tabled) during the same meeting or convention.

> *Example*
> **MEMBER:** I move to resume consideration concerning the appropriation of $100,000 for a public information campaign that was postponed temporarily yesterday.
>
> **PRESIDING OFFICER** (after motion is seconded): It has been moved and seconded that we resume consideration of the motion to appropriate $100,000 for a public information program. If it is desired, the secretary will please read this motion. . . . Those in favor of resuming consideration of the motion that we appropriate $100,000 for a public information campaign, say Aye. . . . Those opposed, please say No. . . . The motion carries, and the motion that we appropriate $100,000 for a public information campaign is open for discussion.

ONLY AT SAME MEETING OR CONVENTION

The motion to resume consideration applies only to a main motion that has been postponed temporarily (tabled) at the current meeting or convention. At a later meeting, the substance of the temporarily postponed motion may be brought up as a new main motion.

PRECEDENCE OVER MAIN MOTIONS

The motion to resume consideration is unique in that, even though it can be proposed only when no other motion is pending, it takes precedence over all other new main motions. If, at the same time, other members want to make other main motions, preference is given to the member asking for a resumption of consideration over all members proposing other main motions.

WHAT IS RESUMED?

Consideration is resumed on exactly the motion that

was postponed. If the motion to postpone temporarily has attached to it amendments and other subsidiary motions, these are all considered, in the same order that they would originally have been considered.

EFFECT

The effect of the motion to resume consideration is that the original main motion, with any attached subsidiary motions, is before the assembly in exactly the same state it was when postponed.

RULES GOVERNING THE MOTION
TO RESUME CONSIDERATION

1. The speaker cannot be interrupted.
2. The motion requires a second.
3. The motion is not debatable.
4. The motion is not amendable.
5. The motion applies to the main motion.
6. The motion can have applied to it no other motions.
7. The motion requires a majority vote for passage.
8. The motion takes precedence over all other new main motions.

Chapter 7

Subsidiary Motions

Subsidiary motions change the main motion or the manner in which it is handled. Subsidiary motions are usually applied to the main motion, but some may be applied to other motions.

The most frequently used subsidiary motions are

Postpone temporarily (table)
Vote immediately
Limit debate
Postpone definitely
Refer for a decision
Refer for report
Amend

Motion to Amend

The purpose of the motion to amend is to change a motion that is being considered by the assembly so that it expresses, as closely as possible, exactly the will of the members. The most frequently used methods of amending a motion are by addition, by deletion, by striking and inserting, and by substitution.

Examples

Original Motion

MEMBER: I move that the annual dues for regular and honorary members of this association be increased to $100, effective 1 January of the next year.

Amendment by Addition

MEMBER: I move to amend the motion by the addition of the words "and complimentary" before the word "members."

PRESIDING OFFICER (after hearing a second): It has been moved and seconded to amend the motion by inserting the words "and complimentary" before the word "members." The motion, as amended, would read that the annual dues for regular, honorary, and complimentary members of this association be increased to $100, effective 1 January of the next year. Is there discussion on the amendment? . . . Those in favor of the amendment, say Aye. . . . Those opposed, No. . . . The amendment is carried. . . . Is there discussion on the motion as amended?

Amendment by Deletion

MEMBER: I move to amend the motion by deleting the word "honorary."

PRESIDING OFFICER (after hearing a second): It has been moved and seconded to amend the motion by deleting the word "honorary." The motion, if amended, would read that the annual dues for regular and complimentary members of this association be increased to $100, effective 1 January of the next year.

Amendment by Striking and Inserting

MEMBER: I move to amend the motion by striking the words "1 January of the next year" and inserting in their place the word "immediately."

PRESIDING OFFICER (after hearing a second): It has been moved and seconded to amend the motion by striking the words "1 January of the next year" and inserting in their place the word "immediately." The motion, if amended, would read that the annual dues for regular and complimentary members of this association be increased to $100, effective immediately.

Amendment by Substitution

MEMBER: I move to amend the motion by substituting for it the following motion: I move that the president of our association be requested to appoint a committee to study our dues structure, this committee to report at our next meeting.

PRESIDING OFFICER (after hearing a second): It has been moved and seconded to amend the motion that the annual dues for regular and complimentary members be increased to $100, effective immediately, by substituting for it a new motion that the president of our association be requested to appoint a committee to study our dues structure, this committee to report at our next meeting.

WHICH MOTIONS CAN BE AMENDED?

The test that determines whether a motion may be amended is whether the motion can be stated in language which makes the motion substantially different. The subsidiary motions to postpone temporarily (table) and to vote immediately are not amendable.

The only motions that may be amended without restriction are the main motion and the motion to amend.

Four subsidiary motions are open to restricted amendment. The motions to limit debate and to postpone definitely may be amended as to time. The motion to refer for decision may be amended as to instructions and as to the time the action taken is to be reported back to the assembly. The motion to refer for report may be amended as to the group the motion is to be referred to, the number of members of the group, and method of selecting the group (if it is not a standing committee, commission, or board), instructions to the group, and the time the motion is to be reported back to the assembly.

AMENDMENTS MUST BE GERMANE

Amendments must be germane to and have significant bearing upon the subject of the pending motion that the amendments intend to change.

Example of an appropriate motion to amend
MEMBER: I move that the motion that the officers of the association investigate the availability of directors' and officers' liability insurance be amended by the addition of the words "and that our insurance carrier be retained to assist them." This amendment is closely related to the intent of the motion, which is to procure directors' and officers' liability insurance.

Example of an inappropriate motion to amend
MEMBER: I move that the motion that the officers of the association investigate the availability of directors' and officers' liability insurance be amended by the addition of the words "and that the compensation paid to our officers and directors be increased 10 percent effective immediately."

Though one could argue that directors and officers without liability insurance should receive additional compensation, this amendment is not germane to the idea of the motion and would be ruled not germane. The chair might suggest to the assembly that the two ideas are related and suggest to the proposer of the inappropriate motion that his motion could be in order after the current issue is settled.

AMENDMENTS CANNOT CHANGE TYPE OF MOTION

An amendment cannot change one type of motion into another type. For example, if a member moves that all pending questions be referred to the board of trustees, it would be out of order for another member to move that the motion be amended by striking the words "be referred to the board of trustees" and inserting in their place the words "be postponed until this afternoon." Though the second member's intention may be appropriate, namely to have the assembly gather more information before referring the matter to the board of trustees, the method is not only cumbersome but incorrect. It changes the motion to refer to a motion to postpone definitely, and such a change is never proper. Even though the motion to postpone definitely has a higher precedence, one should not attempt to amend a current motion to accomplish postponement but rather should move to postpone definitely. This would be much simpler and more appropriate, and the chair would advise that the issue then is not to amend but to postpone definitely.

AMENDMENTS MAY BE HOSTILE

An amendment may not only change the motion drastically, it can reverse the intent and still be appropriate. For example, the motion that the members convey to the president their displeasure at his recent testimony on the question of abortion might be amended by striking the words "their displeasure" and inserting the words "their pleasure and appreciation." This amendment would be germane, though it reverses the original intent, since it relates to the subject of the motion, which is to express the assembly's feeling about the testimony.

Though the intent of a motion can be reversed by amendment (as above), the amendment cannot simply change an affirmative statement to a negative statement. For example, a motion that the members assume the expenses of the president's attendance at the annual meeting cannot be changed simply by inserting the words "do not" before the word "assume." The chair would rule this out of order and remind the assembly that the proper procedure for those who disfavor the motion is to vote against it.

RANK OF AMENDMENTS

There are only two ranks of amendments.

> Amendments applied to the original motion are amendments of the first rank (primary amendments).
>
> Amendments to a pending amendment are amendments of the second rank (secondary amendments).

Amendments of either rank must relate directly to the motion or the amendment to which they are affixed.

Only one amendment of each rank can be pending at any time. When an amendment to a motion is pending (first rank), another amendment of the same rank is not in order. However, an amendment to the amendment (second rank) is in order.

Following the adoption or the defeat of an amendment of either rank, another amendment of the same rank is in order. There is no limit on the number of amendments, either first rank or second rank, that may be offered during the debate, provided that at all times only one amendment of each rank be pending.

> *Example*
>
> **MEMBER:** I move that this association hold a reception for our retiring executive vice president at the Fairmont Hotel on 15 January.
>
> **SECOND MEMBER** (after a second and during the discussion): I move that this be amended by the addition of the words "and that the presidents of all affiliated state associations be invited." [Amendment of the first rank.]
>
> **THIRD MEMBER:** I move that the words "Hilton Hotel" be substituted for the words "Fairmont Hotel." [Amendment out of order because the motion already has an amendment of the first rank.]
>
> **FOURTH MEMBER:** I move to amend the amendment by substitution of the words "all officers" for the word "presidents," so that the amend-

ment shall read, "and that the officers of all affiliated state associations be invited." [Amendment of the second rank.]

Since there is no amendment of the second rank pending, the latter amendment is in order. Once the pending amendment has been disposed of, the motion, as amended, can have affixed to it an amendment of the first order, such as substituting "Hilton Hotel" for "Fairmont Hotel."

DEBATE OF AMENDMENTS

When there is an amendment and also an amendment to the amendment, discussion is first taken on the amendment to the amendment. After this has been disposed of, discussion is then held on the amendment. After that has been disposed of, discussion on the motion or on the motion as amended (as the case may be) is appropriate. In all cases, debate must be limited to the pending issue. That is, if debate is on the amendment to the amendment, it is not proper to discuss the amendment or the motion. Likewise, when an amendment of the first rank is being discussed, discussion should be limited to this amendment and not to the motion itself. It is proper, if desired, for a member to state, "If the pending amendment is defeated, I am prepared to offer another," and for him or her to state briefly the substance of the idea. This alerts the membership that another alternative is possible should they want to defeat the pending amendment and open up the opportunity of another approach.

An amendment to a debatable motion is itself debatable.

AMENDMENT BY SUBSTITUTION

If the wording of a motion is thought not to be clear and several amendments of addition might be required to clarify it, it may be better to offer an amendment of substitution. The substitute amendment must be germane to the general topic, though it may differ vastly from the original amendment.

An amendment by substitution is a form of primary amendment, and consequently it is subject only to an amendment of the second rank. It applies only to main motions. For example, if a motion has been made and seconded that the president be requested to appoint a committee to recommend an appropriate way in which the retiring executive vice president be honored, it would be in order for a member to say, "Mr. Chair, I move to substitute for the pending motion a motion that our next regularly scheduled meeting be made a dinner meeting, that spouses of the members be invited, and that the program be dedicated to honoring our retiring executive vice president." This would be germane to the central idea, that of honoring the retiring executive vice president, and would make specific recommendations which could be acted on rather than waiting for a committee to be formed, to meet, and to bring back its recommendations.

FILLING IN BLANKS

A member may sometimes be undecided about the exact date or numbers that he or she wants to apply to a motion and appeals for help to the assembly by leaving "blanks" in the motion. After the motion is presented and before it is seconded, suggested dates or numbers are received, after which a vote is taken on each suggestion in order of its proposal. Each member is allowed to vote for or against each suggestion, and the one receiving the highest affirmative vote is inserted in the blank. Once the blanks have been filled, a second of the completed motion is made and a vote is taken.

Example

MEMBER: I move that the association have a reception for our retiring executive vice president to be held at _____ hotel on _____ May.

PRESIDING OFFICER: Suggestions are in order for the name of the hotel in which the reception will be held. When two or more hotels are suggested, each will be voted on in order of its proposal.

PRESIDING OFFICER (after the hotel has been voted on): Suggested dates on which the reception will be held are in order. When two or more dates are suggested, each will be voted on in order of its proposal.

PRESIDING OFFICER (after the date has been voted on): It has been moved that the association have a reception for our retiring executive vice president at the Marriott Hotel on 1 May. Is there a second? . . . Is there discussion? . . . All in favor of the motion to hold the reception for our retiring executive vice president at the Marriott Hotel on 1 May, please say Aye. . . . Those opposed, No. . . . The motion is carried.

ACCEPTING AMENDMENTS BY CONSENT

If a member proposes an amendment to a pending motion and the original proposer wishes to accept the amendment, he or she can save time by announcing acceptance of the amendment: "Madam Chair, I accept the amendment."

The consent of the seconder is not necessary, as the proposer of the motion, by accepting the amendment, becomes the seconder.

The presiding officer then asks if there is objection to acceptance, and, if none is made, the presiding officer then states that the motion is amended by general consent. If there is objection, the amendment is voted on in the usual manner.

AMENDMENTS ADHERE TO MOTION

A main motion and all pending amendments are handled as one piece of business. That is, if the motion is referred or postponed, all pending amendments go with it. When the main motion again comes before the assembly (by report of committee, recall, or termination of postponement), the matter before the assembly is the main motion and all amendments.

VOTING ON AMENDMENTS

Amendments are discussed (if debatable) and voted on in the reverse order of their proposal. Thus, discussion and vote on an amendment to the amendment (second rank) is taken first. Then debate and vote is taken on the amendment (first rank), whether it has been amended by the previous action or not. Finally, discussion and vote are taken on the motion, whether it has been amended or not.

It must be constantly remembered that a vote adopting an amendment does not adopt the motion; a specific vote on the adoption of the motion as amended is required.

VOTE REQUIRED FOR PASSAGE OF AMENDMENTS

An amendment, whether it be to a motion (first rank) or to an amendment (second rank), requires a majority vote. The motion to which the amendment is adhered may itself require a higher vote for adoption.

An amendment to the constitution or to the bylaws of an association requires the vote provided for in those documents. However, proposed amendments to a constitution or bylaws require only a majority vote. That is, passage of a proposed amendment by a simple majority allows the assembly to then move on to consideration of actually revising the constitution or bylaws in the manner in which those individual documents prescribe.

AMENDMENTS TO CHANGE ACTION ALREADY TAKEN

Even after a main motion has been passed, it is subject to being amended by a new main motion providing a change. An amendment to the constitution, bylaws, or rules of an association adopted previously by a majority vote requires the vote and method of handling (delay, notice, and so on) provided in the document to which it pertains.

EFFECT

The vote to amend changes the motion as the amendment provides.

RULES GOVERNING THE MOTION
TO AMEND

1. The speaker cannot be interrupted.
2. The motion requires a second.
3. The motion is debatable when applied to a debatable motion.
4. The motion is amendable.
5. The motion applies to rewordable motions: the main motion and the motions to amend, to refer for report, to refer for decision, to postpone definitely, to limit debate, and to recess.
6. The motion can have applied to it the motions to vote immediately and to limit debate.
7. The motion requires a majority vote for passage (even if the motion to which it applies requires a higher vote).
8. The motion takes precedence over the main motion.

Motion to Refer for Report

The purpose of the motion to refer for report is to transfer to another body of the organization (such as a committee, council, task force, or board of trustees) the opportunity and responsibility of studying the proposal and reporting back to the assembly with recommendations. Some large organizations have a standing rule that all referrals from its legislative assembly will go to the board of trustees for further referral to the appropriate group(s). This does not prevent a member, in moving to refer, from specifying a body that he or she wants to consider the proposal, though if the motion to refer for report concerns a subject that is within the jurisdiction of a standing committee, it is ordinarily referred to that group by general consent.

The assembly may specify when it wants the report, as "and report back at our next annual meeting." If the time of reporting is not specified, the receiving body should report as soon as it has concluded its work.

If the motion does not specify which group should report on an issue, the chair may ask the assembly to determine the details (either before or after the motion to refer is approved). Alternatively, the presiding officer has the responsibility to determine those details.

Debate on the motion to refer for report and on amendments to it is limited to a brief discussion as to the advisability of referring or details about the size, membership, method of selection, duties of the committee, and instructions.

If no main motion is pending, the motion to refer is a main motion. An assembly that has referred a motion may at any time consider recalling (withdrawing) the motion back to its jurisdiction for action, different referral, and so on.

EFFECT

The motion to refer for report transfers the referred motion and any pending amendments to an identified body of the association for its study and report with recommendations.

RULES GOVERNING THE MOTION
TO REFER FOR REPORT

1. The speaker cannot be interrupted.
2. The motion requires a second.
3. Debate is limited to a brief discussion as to the group to which the referral is to be made, its size, selection, duties, and instructions.
4. Amendments are restricted to the same details as debate.
5. The motion applies to the main motion.
6. The motion can have applied to it the motions to amend, to vote immediately, and to limit debate.
7. The motion requires a majority vote for passage.
8. The motion takes precedence over the motion to amend.

Motion to Refer for Decision

The purpose of the motion to refer for decision is to transfer to a body authorized to take action the privilege and responsibility of studying and investigating a proposal, making a decision, and taking action, if this is indicated.

Often a matter is of such urgency that an early decision (before the assembly can meet to receive the report and to make the decision itself) is necessary. Consequently, this motion not only transfers the matter for study and investigation; it also authorizes the body to which the matter is referred to make the decision and take action as appropriate. The body to which the matter is referred then reports back to the assembly, usually in informal ways as soon as possible and formally at the next meeting of the assembly.

Debate on the motion to refer for decision or on amendments to it is restricted to brief discussion as to the advisability of referring for decision rather than referring for report or taking other action.

EFFECT

The effect of the motion to refer for decision is to transfer the motion with the request and authority for the body receiving it to make a decision, either affirmative or negative, and to take action as appropriate.

RULES GOVERNING THE MOTION
TO REFER FOR DECISION

1. The speaker cannot be interrupted.
2. The motion requires a second.
3. Debate is limited to the advisability of referring and the group to which referral is to be made.
4. The motion is amendable only as to the group to which referral is to be made.
5. The motion applies to the main motion.
6. The motion can have applied to it the motions to amend, to vote immediately, and to limit debate.
7. The motion requires a majority vote for passage.
8. The motion takes precedence over the motions to refer for report and to amend.

Motion to Postpone Definitely

The purpose of the motion to postpone definitely is to delay further consideration of a pending main motion until a stated time.

Example
MEMBER: I move to postpone the motion until this afternoon and to make it the first item of business in the afternoon session.

POSTPONING DEFINITELY VERSUS POSTPONING TEMPORARILY

The motion to postpone definitely delays consideration of the pending main motion, establishes a definite date or time for its consideration, and may make it either a general or special order for the designated time. Debate is permitted, limited to a brief discussion of the reason for postponement or of the time the motion will be reconsidered.

The motion to postpone definitely is vastly different from the motion to postpone temporarily (table), as the latter motion specifies no time for consideration and is not debatable. The viability of the motion to postpone temporarily terminates at the end of the current meeting or convention unless a motion has been passed to resume consideration (take from the table). Consequently, the motion to postpone temporarily can be used to attempt to terminate consideration, which is not true of the motion to postpone definitely, as a time for consideration is fixed.

A main motion can be postponed definitely only to a meeting or convention that is already scheduled *or* to a time that will allow the motion to be effective, if adopted. For example, a motion to invite the national president to address the next annual meeting cannot be postponed definitely to any time later than the next annual meeting. The motion cannot be used to kill a motion by a delay which defeats the purpose of the motion.

The motion to postpone definitely can be a general or a special order.

GENERAL ORDER

Any main motion postponed definitely to a particular time automatically becomes a general order for that time. At the specified time, the presiding officer states the postponed motion to the assembly for immediate consideration. If another matter is pending, the presiding officer states the general order to the assembly as soon as the pending matter is disposed of. The motion to postpone definitely by general order requires a majority vote.

SPECIAL ORDER

If the assembly votes to make consideration of the postponed motion a special order, at the designated time the matter must be taken up immediately regardless of any other pending business. Any matter which is interrupted by implementation of the special order is put aside until the special order is acted upon, and consideration of the interrupted motion is then resumed. A motion to postpone definitely by special order, since it interrupts pending business, requires a two-thirds vote. At the designated time for implementation of the special order, should the assembly desire not to take up consideration of it, further postponement requires a two-thirds vote.

If a main motion is postponed definitely to the same meeting or convention or to a later meeting or convention, as either a general or special order, but the time or place in the order of business is not specified, it is considered under unfinished business at the designated session. For example, a main motion might be postponed definitely until the opening of the afternoon session tomorrow, until 4:00 P.M. today, or until after the presidential address. Failing such direction, the matter is considered under unfinished business in the designated session.

If a motion that was postponed definitely is not taken up at the designated meeting, it is considered as unfinished business at the next meeting.

If there is not a pending main motion and a motion is made to postpone definitely a future item on the agenda, the motion to postpone definitely is a main motion.

EFFECT

Postponing definitely delays consideration of the pending main motion, continues its viability, and fixes a definite time for its consideration.

RULES GOVERNING THE MOTION
TO POSTPONE DEFINITELY

1. The speaker cannot be interrupted.
2. The motion requires a second.
3. Debate is limited to brief discussion as to the reasons for and/or the time of postponement.
4. The motion is amendable only as to the time the motion will be considered.
5. The motion applies to the main motion.
6. The motion can have applied to it the motions to amend, to vote immediately, and to limit debate.
7. The motion requires a majority vote for passage to postpone definitely by general order and a two-thirds vote for passage to postpone definitely by special order.
8. The motion takes precedence over the motions to amend, to refer for report, and to refer for decision.

Motion to Limit or Extend Debate

The purpose of the motion to limit or extend debate is to determine the time that will be devoted to discussion of a pending motion or the time each speaker may discuss the motion. Limits previously imposed may be modified or removed by the same motion.

Examples

> **MEMBER:** Because of the heavy agenda and the limited time of this meeting, I move that for every session each speaker be limited to a total of three minutes per discussion.

> **MEMBER:** I move to limit debate on this question to a total time of thirty minutes.

> **MEMBER:** Because of the importance of this issue, I move that the previous limitation of three minutes per speaker be extended to four minutes, for this issue alone.

LIMITATIONS ON DEBATE

An assembly may control debate on a pending question in any way it chooses. However, to restrict the freedom of debate requires a two-thirds majority.

The most common limitations concern the length of time allocated for discussion of the motion, the number of speakers who may participate for each side, the length of time allocated to each member, and the specific restriction on the time of nonmembers (such as outside experts, resource individuals, and so on).

Example

> **MEMBER:** Because of the large number of our members who wish to speak on this subject, and the need for expert testimony from others, I move that nonmembers who are granted privilege of the floor also be limited to four minutes.

Limits may be placed for an entire meeting, for a particular session, for the pending motion, or even for the pending amendment to the motion. Such restrictions are subject to revision, if the assembly chooses.

The motion to limit or extend debate can be amended in a limited form, one that is germane but does not conflict with the intent of the motion. For example, if the motion to limit discussion to thirty minutes is pending, an amendment may be proposed to add the words "and that the number of speakers on each side be limited to three."

If no main motion is pending and a motion is made to limit or extend debate on a future motion, the motion to limit or extend debate becomes a main motion. The limits or extension applied to a main motion are applicable only during the current meeting or convention. If the main motion is postponed until another meeting, the limits or extension are not applicable.

The motion to limit or extend debate regulates discussion of the pending motion or a future motion. It may also be used to remove limitations previously placed.

RULES GOVERNING THE MOTION TO LIMIT OR EXTEND DEBATE

1. The speaker cannot be interrupted.
2. The motion requires a second.
3. The motion is debatable, limited to the time, number of speakers, and so on.
4. The motion is amendable in a limited form.
5. The motion applies only to debatable motions.
6. The motion can have applied to it the motion to amend.
7. The motion requires a two-thirds vote for passage.
8. The motion takes precedence over the motions to amend, to refer for report, to refer for decision, and to postpone definitely.

Motion to Vote Immediately

The purpose of the motion to vote immediately is to close discussion on the pending question or questions and to bring them to an immediate vote.

Historically, there has been great confusion over the clearest and most appropriate way to end discussion and have the assembly move to a decisive vote. Earlier, the motion "I move the previous question" was used, or simply the shouted "Question." More recently there has been greater use of the motion to close debate to accomplish the same purpose. Currently the motion to vote immediately is the proper form.

What the assembly really wants to do is vote on the issue, and to do this debate has to be stopped. It is clearer for the assembly to grasp that if the motion to vote immediately is passed, all debate has been stopped than to understand that the motion to close debate will bring up an immediate vote. The clearest and most widely used form of bringing an issue to the vote is to use the motion to vote immediately.

The motion to vote immediately is very powerful, in that it stops all further discussion (except for a motion to postpone temporarily), and consequently requires a two-thirds vote.

WHEN CAN THE MOTION BE USED?

Technically, the motion to vote immediately is in order anytime during the discussion of a motion. However, it cannot be combined with another motion, as "I move that dues be increased $100 per year and that we vote immediately." This obviously would prevent any discussion of the question.

Opportunity for both sides of the question to be discussed must be allowed before a motion to vote immediately is in order. The chair should carefully keep a record of which side(s) have been discussed, to allow the motion to vote immediately at the appropriate time. After both sides of the issue have been discussed, any member may move to vote immediately as his or her only statement.

WHICH MOTIONS AND AMENDMENTS ARE AFFECTED?

If the motion to vote immediately does not specify what exactly is to be voted on, the motion applies only to the immediately pending motion. For example, if a motion has a single amendment attached and discussion is on the amendment, the motion to vote immediately applies to the amendment only.

If it is desired to vote immediately on more than the immediately pending motion, the member must clearly specify the pending motions or amendments to which the motion applies. For example, if there is a pending motion with two pending amendments and the member wants to vote immediately on the amendments (they may be thought to be inconsequential), this must be clearly stated. Otherwise, the vote will be taken only on the amendment of the second order.

"ON ALL PENDING ISSUES"

A member may want to vote on all pending issues, for example, a main motion with amendments, a motion to refer for report, and a motion to refer for decision. He or she must make a motion to vote immediately on all pending issues. If the motion to vote immediately on all pending issues is successful, the voting will be in reverse order—first on the motion to refer for decision, then on the motion to refer for report, then on the amendments, and finally on the motion itself—until an affirmative vote is achieved.

APPLIES TO SAME MEETING ONLY

The effect of the motion to vote immediately terminates with the meeting or convention at which it is adopted. For example, if, after a successful motion to vote immediately, the assembly postpones the main motion temporarily (tables) but resumes consideration of it later in the same meeting or convention, the motion to vote immediately still applies to all motions that have been postponed. This contrasts with a situation in which the assembly votes to postpone the main motion until a later meeting. The motion to vote immediately no longer applies.

PRESIDING OFFICER CAN CLEAR CONFUSION

Any motion made or simply called out without recognition is clearly out of order. However, there are times when it is evident that the assembly wants to vote immediately, as when "Question!" or "Vote immediately!" is called out. The chair can facilitate movement, rather than simply ruling individuals out of order, by asking, "Do I hear a motion to vote immediately?" When there are affirmative answers, the chair obtains a second and proceeds with the vote. Another option the chair has in such a situation is to simply ask if there is objection to voting immediately; if there is none, he or she can proceed by general consent to take the vote.

EFFECT

The effect of the motion to vote immediately is to bring all discussion to an immediate halt and to proceed with a vote.

RULES GOVERNING THE MOTION
TO VOTE IMMEDIATELY

1. The speaker cannot be interrupted.
2. The motion requires a second.

3. The motion is not debatable.
4. The motion is not amendable.
5. The motion applies only to debatable motions.
6. The motion can have applied to it no other motions.
7. The motion requires a two-thirds vote for passage.
8. The motion takes precedence over the motions to amend, to refer for report, to refer for decision, to postpone definitely, and to limit or extend debate.

Motion to Postpone Temporarily (Table)

The purpose of the motion to postpone temporarily is to set aside a pending main motion, which can be taken up for further consideration at any time during the same meeting or convention.

> *Examples*
> **MEMBER:** I move that this motion be postponed temporarily.
>
> **MEMBER:** I move to table the motion.

WHY POSTPONE TEMPORARILY?

The usual reasons for postponing temporarily are that further information will be available at a later time and more appropriate discussion held later or that a more urgent matter has arisen which the assembly wants to discuss in place of the pending motion. Sometimes this motion is used to delay consideration of the main motion in the hope that if it is reconsidered later, more support of a particular position will be available. In earlier times, a subsidiary motion to postpone indefinitely was available and was used as a method of delaying or killing a proposed motion. Most parliamentarians no longer recognize this motion. In its absence, the motion to postpone temporarily is at times used with the same intent.

APPLIES ONLY TO MAIN MOTIONS

This motion applies only to main motions and not to reports, addresses, and other communications.

A motion postponed temporarily sets aside the pending main motion for the duration of the current meeting or convention unless the assembly votes to resume its consideration. Reconsideration is accomplished by the specific main motion to resume consideration (take from table). In the absence of a motion for reconsideration, the matter is mute during the remaining meeting or convention.

Once the motion to postpone temporarily has been voted, the matter cannot be brought up as a new main motion during the same meeting or convention but may be handled as a new main motion at any future meeting or convention.

When a main motion is postponed temporarily, all adhering motions and amendments are postponed with it. When the matter is brought before the assembly for reconsideration, the entire package is handled in the usual order.

A majority vote is required to pass the motion to postpone temporarily.

Because postponing a motion does stop discussion of the matter, some parliamentarians have suggested that when this motion is used for the sole purpose of suppressing debate or killing it, a two-thirds vote be required. This approach would require a presiding officer always to judge correctly the motive of the individual moving to postpone temporarily. Consequently, it is subject to error and possible unfair treatment.

Since a majority vote is required to postpone temporarily, the same majority could vote to defeat such a motion, if their intent was to protect the issue. Postponing temporarily is effective in killing a measure only if the motion is not brought back for consideration, an option the assembly has at all times by only a majority vote. It is ludicrous to suggest a majority vote on this motion on some occasions and a two-thirds vote on other occasions, depending on the judged motive of the proposer.

EFFECT

The effect of the motion to postpone temporarily is to remove from consideration during the current meeting or convention a pending main motion and adhering motions and amendments unless the assembly votes to resume consideration.

RULES GOVERNING THE MOTION
TO POSTPONE TEMPORARILY

1. The speaker cannot be interrupted.
2. The motion requires a second.
3. The motion is not debatable.
4. The motion is not amendable.
5. The motion applies only to main motions.
6. The motion can have no other motion applied to it.
7. The motion requires a majority vote.
8. The motion takes precedence over all other subsidiary motions.

Motion to Recall

This motion is rarely used, but it can be very useful to an assembly at appropriate times.

The purpose of the subsidiary motion to recall is to undo a previously adopted motion to refer. The assembly has the right, for any reason, to take back anything it has referred to any constituent group (committee, commission, task force, board of trustees).

The assembly may feel that more immediate action on the matter is necessary, it may wish to apply certain instructions or restrictions to its referral, or it may want to withdraw the matter from further consideration.

RULES GOVERNING THE MOTION TO RECALL

1. The speaker cannot be interrupted.
2. The motion requires a second.
3. The motion is debatable only as to the advisability of recall.
4. The motion is not amendable.
5. The motion applies only to the motion to refer.
6. The motion can have applied to it the motions to vote immediately and to limit debate.
7. The motion requires a majority vote for passage.
8. The motion takes precedence over the motions to refer for decision, to refer for report, and to amend.

Chapter 8

Privileged Motions

Privileged motions have the highest rank of all motions with precedence because they terminate or interrupt meetings. Necessity determines the precedence of all motions, and the urgency of privileged motions is based on the belief that a deliberative body should not be kept in session against its will. Consequently, there are only two privileged motions: recess and adjourn.

Privileged motions are privileged when they are proposed when a main motion is pending. If they are proposed when no main motion is pending, they become main motions.

The question of privilege, which is a request and becomes a motion only if denied, should not be confused with privileged motions. Question of privilege has to do with the rights, comfort, or convenience of the assembly or of at least one of its members, not with keeping the assembly in session.

Motion to Recess

The purpose of the motion to recess is to provide an interlude in a meeting. The length of the recess or the establishment of a definite time for resuming deliberations should be set.

There are many reasons why at times it is necessary or convenient to recess a meeting. The members may be tired, a committee report may be delayed, the election committee may be counting ballots, the hall may be needed for other purposes, and so forth.

Examples

MEMBER: I move that we recess for thirty minutes.

MEMBER: Because it is necessary to prepare this hall for the president's reception this evening, I move that we recess until eight o'clock tomorrow morning.

DIFFERENCES BETWEEN RECESS AND ADJOURN

A motion to recess suspends the current meeting until a later time. An unqualified motion to adjourn terminates the meeting.

A motion to recess and a motion to adjourn to a continued meeting are actually the same. Each provides the interlude with which the meeting is interrupted.

When a recessed meeting reconvenes, the assembly resumes its work at the point at which it was interrupted by the motion to recess. When an assembly reconvenes following an adjournment, it begins an entirely new meeting and agenda.

LIMITATION ON MOTION TO RECESS

The motion to recess takes effect immediately unless the motion specifies otherwise. Though a recess is usually brief or overnight, there is no specific limitation on its length except that a recess cannot extend beyond the time set for the next regular meeting. In a convention, recess cannot extend beyond the time set for the next business meeting or beyond the time set for adjournment of the convention.

The motion to recess may be amended as to the time or duration of the recess. Debate on a motion to recess is restricted to the need, duration, or time of reconvening.

A motion for a recess set for a future time is not a privileged motion but rather a main motion.

EFFECT

The effect of the motion to recess is to suspend the activities of the meeting until the time stated for reconvening.

RULES GOVERNING THE MOTION TO RECESS

1. The speaker cannot be interrupted.
2. The motion requires a second.
3. Debate must be limited to the need, time, or duration of recess.
4. The motion is amendable only as to the time or duration of the recess.
5. The motion applies to no other motion.
6. The motion can have applied to it only the limited motion to amend.
7. The motion to recess requires a majority vote.
8. The motion to recess takes precedence over all motions except the motion to adjourn.

Motion to Adjourn

The purpose of the motion to adjourn is to terminate a meeting or convention. There are two forms of the motion to adjourn: the qualified and the unqualified forms.

UNQUALIFIED FORM

The unqualified form is a privileged motion only when a main motion is pending and only if it is stated as an unqualified motion that would take effect immediately if passed. The unqualified motion may be proposed at any time except that it cannot interrupt a speaker or the counting of a vote. However, if the vote is by ballot and all ballots have been collected, the assembly may adjourn while the ballots are being counted.

QUALIFIED FORM

Qualified motions to adjourn are main motions, subject to all the rules of main motions. Even the unqualified motion to adjourn, if proposed when no main motion is pending, becomes a main motion.

Examples

Unqualified Form (Privileged Motion)
MEMBER: I move that we adjourn.

MEMBER: I move that the 100th Annual Meeting of the North Carolina Medical Society now adjourn.

Qualified Form (Main Motion)
MEMBER: I move that we adjourn in thirty minutes.

MEMBER: I move that this meeting adjourn to a continued meeting to be held at nine o'clock on Thursday morning. [Same as recess.]

MEMBER: Because of the travel requirements of many of our members, I move that we adjourn at four o'clock this afternoon.

COMPLETING BUSINESS PRIOR TO ADJOURNMENT

When a motion to adjourn is made, it is the duty of the presiding officer to make certain that no important business is pending before calling for a vote on the motion. If the chair or any member knows of important matters that should be considered, these should be called to the attention of the assembly. For example, if the fiscal year is about to begin and the annual budget for it has not been approved, it is essential that this be done. In such a situation, the presiding officer usually asks the proposer of the motion to adjourn to withdraw the motion until the essential business has been completed. Though members will almost invariably comply with this request, as always the assembly has the right to do what it desires, and the vote on adjournment must be taken if requested or if a proposed motion is not withdrawn.

ADJOURNMENT TO A CONTINUED MEETING

When an assembly cannot complete all of its important work in the time prescribed, it is advisable and often necessary to continue the meeting at a later, definite time. The motion to adjourn the meeting until a later time (which is actually a recess) is a qualified motion to adjourn and thus a main motion. In this motion, it must be stated clearly that the meeting is to be a continuation of the present meeting and the place and time for the adjourned meeting to reconvene must be clearly understood. Since this is a continuation of the same meeting, no special notice to the membership is required unless stipulated in the bylaws.

WHEN ADJOURNMENT WOULD DISSOLVE

Though an unqualified motion to adjourn is a privileged motion, this is excepted when an unqualified motion to adjourn is made which would have the effect of dissolving the organization. In this instance the motion to adjourn is a main motion, governed by the rules of a main motion.

The critical fact that no provision for another meeting has been made and that the assembly will, in effect, be dissolving the organization by adopting the motion should be called to the attention of the assembly by the presiding officer. The assembly should understand that in addition to moving for adjournment, the pending motion also moves for dissolution of the organization. A motion which has the effect of dissolving the group or of closing the convention is called adjournment sine die, or adjournment without day (being set for meeting).

VOTING ON ADJOURNMENT

The decision to adjourn cannot be made by the presiding office, only by the assembly. Only when no quorum is present can the presiding officer arbitrarily declare adjournment.

Even after a successful vote on the motion to adjourn, the meeting is not ended until the presiding officer announces the vote and declares adjournment. However, a formal vote is not always necessary. A perceptive presiding officer, knowing that the agenda has been completed and the time for adjournment has arrived, may ask, "Is there further business to come before the assembly?" If there appears to be none, the presiding officer senses that the assembly has in fact voted for adjournment and states, "If not, hearing no objection, the meeting is adjourned."

Because of the potential confusion about motions to adjourn, the presiding officer has the responsibility of making sure, if necessary by rephrasing, that the intent of the motion is clear. It is good practice for the presiding officer, in declaring any meeting adjourned, to clearly announce the time and place of the next meeting.

ADJOURNMENT AT PREVIOUSLY MENTIONED TIME

When a previously determined time for adjournment arrives, whether set by a previous motion, by adoption of the program agenda, or by rule, it is the responsibility of the presiding officer to interrupt the proceedings and to state that the time determined for adjournment has arrived. It is then in order for action to be taken by a motion to adjourn, a motion to set another time for adjournment, or, if it is a rules-required adjournment, a motion to suspend the rule requiring adjournment.

HANDLING BUSINESS INTERRUPTED BY ADJOURNMENT

In a meeting, business interrupted by adjournment is considered as the first item under unfinished business at the next meeting.

In a convention, business interrupted by adjournment becomes moot, except for an item that was postponed definitely to a later meeting or unless a committee, task force, or other group has had business referred to it with the request for report at the next convention.

EFFECT

The effect of the motion to adjourn is to terminate a meeting or a convention.

RULES GOVERNING THE MOTION TO ADJOURN

1. The speaker cannot be interrupted.
2. The motion requires a second.
3. The motion is not debatable.
4. The motion is not amendable.
5. The motion applies to no other motion.
6. The motion can have applied to it no other motion.
7. The motion requires a majority vote for passage.
8. The motion takes precedence over all other motions.

Chapter 9

Incidental (Nonprecedented) Motions

Another group of motions, none of which have precedence, helps to protect the rights of members. These nonprecedented motions also facilitate the manner in which issues are considered and debated by the assembly. They are known as *incidental motions,* as they do not deal directly with the issues with which the assembly concerns itself but rather deal with how the assembly handles the issues.

Such motions, if successful, will change the immediate action of the assembly. Consequently, they must be decided immediately. The three most frequently used incidental motions are

Appeal
Suspend rules
Consider informally

Motion to Appeal

The purpose of the motion to appeal is to subject the ruling of the presiding officer to examination by the assembly. Any member, suspecting that the presiding officer has been inaccurate, inappropriate, mistaken, or unfair in the ruling may appeal that ruling to the members of the assembly.

Example
MEMBER (immediately after the decision of the chair has been announced and without waiting for recognition): I appeal from the decision of the chair.

The presiding officer states the reason for the ruling and allows the member to state his or her reasons for the appeal. After appropriate discussion by the members, the vote is taken, not on the appeal, but on sustaining the decision of the presiding officer.

Example
PRESIDING OFFICER: Those in favor of sustaining the decision of the chair, say Aye. . . . Those

opposed, No. . . . The decision of the chair is sustained [or overruled].

If no main motion is pending, the motion to appeal is a main motion.

WHEN CAN AND MUST AN APPEAL BE TAKEN?

Any decision of the presiding officer involving judgment or ruling is subject to appeal. Appeals may not be made on statements of fact, existing laws, established rules, or the results of a vote by ballot count.

An appeal must be made immediately after the presiding officer's decision has been announced. If other business has intervened, an appeal is not in order. However, if another member has obtained the floor, the challenging member need not wait for recognition and may interrupt the proceedings to call for the appeal.

MOTION TO APPEAL IS DEBATABLE

An appeal requires a second and is debatable since it may involve matters of great importance to the assembly. The presiding officer states the reason for the ruling, without leaving the chair, and the challenging member states the reasons for the appeal. If either the presiding officer or the challenging member is convinced of the other's argument, the chair may change his or her ruling or the member may withdraw the appeal. If this does not occur, the matter is debated and a vote is taken.

VOTING ON AN APPEAL

The presiding officer must always state the question in the form "Those in favor of sustaining the decision of the chair. . . ." The vote is always on sustaining (or not sustaining) the decision of the chair. It is never on the appeal itself.

The presiding officer's ruling is sustained by either a majority vote or by a tie vote. A majority voting in the negative (against sustaining) is necessary to override the chair decision.

EFFECT

The effect of the motion to appeal is to sustain the ruling if there is an affirmative majority or a tie vote, or to overrule it if there is a majority vote in the negative.

1. The speaker can be interrupted, but it must be done immediately.
2. The motion requires a second.
3. The motion is debatable.
4. The motion is not amendable.
5. The motion applies to no other motion but to rulings of the chair.
6. The motion can have applied to it the motions to vote immediately and to limit debate.
7. The motion requires a negative majority vote (a vote to overrule the chair's ruling) for passage.

Motion to Suspend the Rules

The purpose of the motion to suspend the rules is to allow an assembly to take some action which would otherwise be prevented by the rules of parliamentary procedure, by a program previously adopted, or by the rules of the organization. It makes inoperative temporarily the obstacle which otherwise would prevent the assembly from accomplishing its will. Its effect expires when that action is completed.

Example:

MEMBER: I move to suspend the rules so that we might hear an urgent message from our president at this time.

PRESIDING OFFICER: If there is no objection, the rules will be suspended to allow us to receive an urgent message from our president.

MEMBER: I move to suspend the rules to receive the report of the Special Committee on Arrangements before the regular standing committee reports.

PRESIDING OFFICER: If there is no objection, the rules will be suspended to permit the report of the Special Committee on Arrangements to be heard now. Will the chair of that committee please proceed with the committee report?

MEMBER: Mr. President, I move we suspend the rule requiring a quorum so that we might begin our work.

PRESIDING OFFICER: The rule requiring the presence of a quorum to conduct business legally cannot be suspended. Therefore, the motion is out of order.

WHICH RULES CAN AND CANNOT BE SUSPENDED?

Only procedural rules may be suspended.

Members may not be deprived of their rights by suspension of the rules. Basic rules of parliamentary law such as those that relate to quorum, advance notice of meeting, voting methods, and requirements cannot be suspended.

A rule in the bylaws cannot be suspended unless the bylaws permit the suspension of certain bylaws governing the method or order of considering business. A rule stated in the charter, a statute, the constitution, or the bylaws cannot be suspended.

RESTRICTIONS ON SUSPENSION OF RULES

The motion to suspend the rules is in order when a motion is pending, if its purpose is related to that motion. Otherwise, the motion is in order when no motion is pending.

Rules may be suspended only for a specific purpose and only for the time necessary to accomplish the action. Consequently, a suspended rule becomes effective as soon as the purpose for which it was suspended has been accomplished.

EFFECT

The effect of the motion to suspend the rules is to allow an assembly to take a specified action which otherwise would be impossible under its procedural rules.

RULES GOVERNING THE MOTION
TO SUSPEND THE RULES

1. The speaker cannot be interrupted.
2. The motion requires a second.
3. The motion is not debatable.
4. The motion is not amendable.
5. The motion applies to no other motion.
6. The motion can have applied to it no other motions.
7. The motion requires a two-thirds vote for passage.

Motion to Consider Informally

The purpose of the motion to consider informally is to allow an assembly to discuss an issue without the restrictions of parliamentary rules. It can be used if no motion is pending in the hope that unrestricted discussion will form a consensus supporting the substance and the language of the motion that evolves. It also can be used even though a motion is under consideration. The pending motion is considered informally until the members decide to vote on it. This vote terminates the informal consideration.

Sometimes the assembly desires or urgently needs to develop a position and there is not sufficient time to refer the matter to a committee and await its report. Informal consideration allows the group to do its best, collective work in a brief period of time. Should no agreement be reached during the informal consideration, a motion is needed to terminate informal consideration.

Example

MEMBER: Our organization is in serious and urgent need of sending a small group of our best qualified and most representative members to consult with the governor on several important matters. To choose those who we feel are best qualified to present our views and who would be most acceptable to this body, I move that we consider informally the selection of this group.

PRESIDING OFFICER: Is there a second? . . . We will vote on the question of having informal consideration of the selection of our most representative members to consult with the governor. All those favoring the motion, say Aye. . . . Those opposed, No. . . . The motion is carried. The floor is now open for informal discussion.

This motion has been confused with the obsolete motion of committee of the whole, in which the presiding officer relinquished the chair, all votes were considered to be committee votes and not binding, and the temporary chair reported back to the assembly after it had officially gone back into session. Obviously, informal consideration is a much improved method of achieving the same goal and, though rarely used, has a definite place in parliamentary law.

EFFECT

The effect of the motion to consider informally is to allow an assembly to have full and unrestricted discussion of a matter without the limitations of parliamentary law.

RULES GOVERNING THE MOTION
TO CONSIDER INFORMALLY

1. The speaker cannot be interrupted.
2. The motion requires a second.
3. The motion is not debatable.
4. The motion is not amendable.
5. The motion applies to the main motion.
6. The motion can have applied to it no other motions.
7. The motion requires a majority vote for passage.

Chapter 10

Requests

Requests are very different from motions. The distinction between motions and requests should be understood clearly by all who work in parliamentary procedure. The confusion results from the fact that previously requests have been called and have been handled as incidental motion—which they are not.

Requests are the expression of the rights of all members. They are examples of the protection that members possess and may express at almost any time.

Requests are of two types: conditional and mandatory.

Conditional requests are requests which any member may make and which may be granted by the presiding officer. If a conditional request is not granted, or if there is objection by any member, the request then becomes a motion, requires no second, is not debatable or amendable, and must be voted on immediately. The most frequently used conditional requests are

Question of privilege
Withdraw motion
Division of the question

All except division of the question may interrupt the speaker.

Mandatory requests must be granted by the presiding officer, and any member may interrupt the speaker to make the request. Point of order or parliamentary inquiry may be made at any time; division of the assembly may be requested following any indecisive vote. Thus, the most frequently used mandatory requests are

Point of order
Parliamentary inquiry
Division of the assembly

The rules governing requests are discussed in the following sections and are presented in Table 4 on pages 78–79 and on the rear endpapers.

Table 4 *Rules Governing Requests*

Requests	Interrupt Speaker?	Second Needed?	Debate Allowed?
Conditional Requests[a]			
Question of Privilege	Yes	No	No
Withdraw Motion	Yes	No	No
Division of Question	No	No	No
Mandatory Requests[b]			
Point of Order	Yes	NA[c]	NA
Parliamentary Inquiry	Yes	NA	NA
Division of Assembly	Yes	NA	NA

[a] Conditional requests must be granted or voted on immediately.
[b] Mandatory requests must be granted immediately.
[c] NA = Not applicable.

Conditional Requests

QUESTION OF PRIVILEGE

The question of privilege was earlier considered by many parliamentarians as a privileged motion. In fact, it is a request that is usually granted by the chair. On the rare occasion it is not granted, or if there is objection, the request becomes a motion. Since it requires no second and is not debatable, the motion moves immediately to resolution by a vote. The assembly understands more clearly the interruption of debate for a request which may require resolution by a vote than it does a privileged motion which becomes a main motion with special privilege when there is already a main motion under discussion.

Examples

MEMBER (without waiting for recognition): Mr. Chair, I rise to a question of privilege of the assembly.

PRESIDING OFFICER: State your question of privilege.

MEMBER: The rear of the hall is exceedingly warm. May we ask the engineers to turn down the heat?

PRESIDING OFFICER: Your request is granted.

Amend-able?	Motions or Action to Which It Applies	Motions That Can Be Applied to It	Vote Required for Passage
No	None	None	Majority
No	All	None	Majority
No	Main	None	Majority
NA	Any error	None	No vote
NA	All	None	No vote
NA	Indecisive vote	None	No vote

Will the engineers please see that the back of the room is made more comfortable?

MEMBER (without waiting for recognition): I rise to a question of personal privilege.

PRESIDING OFFICER: State your question of privilege.

MEMBER: May I please be excused from attending the remaining portion of our morning session because I have received an urgent request to return to my office?

PRESIDING OFFICER: Your request is granted.

MEMBER (without waiting for recognition): Madam Chair, I rise to request a privilege.

PRESIDING OFFICER: State your request.

MEMBER: Because of the excessive heat in this hall, I request that we move to the next room, as I am told that the temperature there is much more comfortable.

PRESIDING OFFICER: I understand and appreciate your request, but we have only a few minutes more of business to accomplish before lunch. I prefer that we endure the heat, since it would take us much longer to move and then complete our agenda. I respectfully deny your request. Those in favor of moving to the next room immediately, please say Aye. . . . Those opposed to moving immediately, please say No. . . . The motion fails. We will conclude our morning session in this room as quickly as possible and will reconvene this afternoon in the room next to us, on your right.

Any member, for personal privilege or for privilege of the assembly, has the right to make a request at any time, without having to wait for recognition from the chair. Since the issue that is raised must be settled immediately, if the request is not granted or is objected to, it must be voted on immediately. As soon as the request has been decided—either granted or voted on—debate returns to the point at which the request was made and the speaker who was interrupted is given the floor.

Since a question of privilege can be for the individual's benefit or that of the assembly, if two such requests are made the question of privilege relating to the assembly takes precedence over the question of privilege relating to an individual member.

WITHDRAW MOTION

The purpose of the request to withdraw a motion is to enable a member to remove from consideration of the assembly a motion which he or she has proposed. If the motion has not been stated to the assembly by the presiding officer no permission is necessary.

Examples

MEMBER (before the motion has been stated to the assembly and without waiting for recognition): Mr. Chair, I withdraw my motion.

PRESIDING OFFICER: The motion is withdrawn.

MEMBER (after the motion has been stated to the assembly and without waiting for recognition): I ask permission to withdraw my motion.

PRESIDING OFFICER: Permission has been requested to withdraw the motion. Is there objection? . . . There being no objection, the motion is withdrawn.

MEMBER (after the motion has been stated to the assembly and without waiting for recognition): I ask permission to withdraw my motion.

PRESIDING OFFICER: Permission has been requested to withdraw the motion. . . . There is objection. . . . Those in favor of permitting withdrawal of the motion, please say Aye. . . . Those opposed, No. . . . This motion is carried and the motion in question is withdrawn.

Usually permission to withdraw is requested because more urgent business needs early consideration, the desired motion has already been accomplished, the motion was erroneously based or stated, or embarrassment might be produced by discussing the motion. A motion can be withdrawn, with permission, up to the moment the final vote is taken. It may be withdrawn even though other motions affecting it may be pending or debate has been closed. Once withdrawn, all amendments adhering to the motion are also withdrawn.

The motion to withdraw is not debatable, although the proposer should be permitted to state his or her reason(s). It is not amendable and requires a majority vote for passage.

DIVISION OF QUESTION

The purpose of a request for division of the question is to divide a motion that is composed of two or more independent parts into separate motions that may be considered and voted on separately. When a motion contains two or more distinct propositions, any member has the right to request division into separate motions. If the presiding officer agrees that the motion contains at least two propositions, each of which can stand alone as a reasonable motion and each suitable for adoption should the other portion fail, he or she may grant this permission.

Example
MEMBER: I move that the salary of our executive vice president be increased by eight percent for the coming year and that her expenses to the national convention be assumed by the organization.
ANOTHER MEMBER (after being recognized): I request division of the question.
PRESIDING OFFICER: This matter is divisible. Permission to divide the question is granted. We will now consider the first portion, that the

salary of our executive vice president be increased by eight percent for the coming year. [After discussion:] All those favoring this motion, please say Aye. . . . Those opposed, No. . . . The motion carries and the executive vice president's salary will be increased. Now before us is the motion that the organization assume the traveling expenses for our executive vice president to attend the national convention. [After discussion:] All those favoring this motion, please say Aye. . . . All those opposed, No. . . . The motion carries, and the organization will assume the traveling expenses for our executive vice president to attend the national convention.

If the presiding officer believes that the issue is not divisible, or if there is objection, the request is denied.

Example

MEMBER: I move that a campaign for new members be undertaken and if adequate funds are generated from this effort that the traveling expenses of our secretary to the national convention be assumed.

ANOTHER MEMBER (after being recognized): I request division of the question.

PRESIDING OFFICER: This motion is not clearly divisible, and permission to divide the question is denied. The motion has received a second and discussion will be on the entire question.

If the presiding officer rules that a motion is divisible, and if there is objection to the way in which it is proposed to divide the issue, he or any member may propose a different division. These constitute alternative proposals and should be voted on in the order in which they are proposed, with the proposal receiving the largest vote being accepted.

The request to divide a question, though most effective if proposed immediately after introduction of the motion, may be requested at any time, even when a motion to vote immediately is pending. Consequently, this request may not interrupt the speaker, applies only to main motions, and requires a majority vote for passage.

Mandatory Requests

The purpose of point of order is to call the attention of the presiding officer and the assembly to a possible violation of the rules, an omission, or an error in the proceedings and to secure a ruling from the presiding officer. If it appears that the presiding officer has made an error in his or her ruling or in stating it, has failed to enforce a rule or has allowed an error on the part of a member, a point of order may be requested.

Examples

MEMBER (without waiting for recognition): I rise to a point of order.

PRESIDING OFFICER: Please state your point of order.

MEMBER: I believe we failed to vote on the last item.

PRESIDING OFFICER: Your point of order is well taken. We did vote on the previous motion, but I failed to report the result. The motion carried, and we have set adjournment for five o'clock this afternoon.

MEMBER: Point of order!

PRESIDING OFFICER: Please state your point of order.

MEMBER: We had agreed to recess for thirty minutes at ten o'clock. That time has arrived.

PRESIDING OFFICER: Your point is well taken. We stand in recess for thirty minutes.

A point of order must be raised immediately after the possible error or omission occurs. Because of urgency, point of order can be made at any time, may interrupt the speaker, and requires no vote, but it does require a ruling by the chair. The presiding officer may take a few minutes to make his or her ruling or may express uncertainty and refer the matter to the assembly for decision. At this time no discussion is allowed, unless the presiding officer invites it in the belief that it may help all members in their decision.

No appeal may be taken from a decision made by the assembly on a point of order. However, as in any decision of the chair a member may appeal from the decision of the chair on a point of order.

As soon as the point of order has been satisfied, the business of the assembly resumes at the point at which it was interrupted. Point of order relates to a potential error in the procedure, not the comfort of a member or of the assembly, which is better addressed through a question of privilege.

PARLIAMENTARY INQUIRY

The purpose of parliamentary inquiry is to seek the presiding officer's opinion on a matter of parliamentary procedure as it relates to the business at hand. It does not involve a ruling of the chair. It can also be used to ask the presiding officer or the proposer of a motion a clarifying question about the pending motion.

A basic responsibility of the presiding officer is to ensure that at all times the members are aware of and well informed about the pending business of the assembly. Consequently, any member has the right to inquire at any time about a procedure which relates directly to the pending action.

The request for parliamentary inquiry may interrupt a speaker only when it requires an immediate answer. If the chair feels that there is no urgency about it, he or she will deny the request but assure the questioner that an opportunity to ask his or her nonurgent question will be offered at an appropriate time.

Examples

MEMBER: I rise to a parliamentary inquiry.

PRESIDING OFFICER: Please state your inquiry.

MEMBER: Is this motion amendable and would an amendment be in order at this time?

PRESIDING OFFICER: It is amendable and an amendment would be in order.

MEMBER: I rise to a parliamentary inquiry.

PRESIDING OFFICER: Please state your inquiry.

MEMBER: Will the presiding officer please inform the assembly as to the rules of the election this afternoon?

PRESIDING OFFICER: This inquiry has no urgency. I will inform the assembly, following the completion of action on this motion, about our plans for the rest of the day. Please continue with the discussion.

A parliamentary inquiry should always be addressed to the presiding officer and answered by the presiding officer. However, the presiding officer may consult with anyone he or she wishes or ask the members if they have an answer. If this is done, a member consulted or a member who can supply an answer directs this information to the chair, never to the inquiring member, and the presiding officer then responds to the inquiry. All conversation between members should be directed to the chair, never directly from one member to another.

There is no appeal from the chair's response to a parliamentary inquiry or other query, since such a reply is an opinion, not a ruling. However, if the member is told that his or her proposed action is out of order, he or she can still propose it and have the chair rule the action (not the opinion) out of order, which is subject to appeal. Parliamentary inquiry should be limited to the pending action, and the presiding officer should give an opinion on the inquiry. However, the presiding officer does not have the responsibility to answer general, unrelated questions on parliamentary procedure.

A member who is interrupted by parliamentary inquiry, once the inquiry is satisfied, retains the floor and continues his or her debate. The privilege of parliamentary inquiry should never be used or allowed as a means of delaying the proceedings or harassing a member. Repeated appeals or inquiries designed to obstruct the flow of business are never in order.

DIVISION OF THE ASSEMBLY

The purpose of the request for division of the assembly is to verify a vote that has been taken by voice or by raised hands. Any member concerned about the vote may call for a division as soon as the motion is put to a vote and even after the vote has been announced. An alert presiding officer, if the voice vote is indecisive, will immediately ask either for a show of hands or a standing vote. If he or she chooses a show of hands and the vote is still indecisive, he or she will then order a standing vote. A show of hands is not a division of the assembly (though it may demonstrate that one side clearly dominates) and even after this method of voting, if the presiding officer does not immediately move to a standing vote, any member may request it. However, this privilege should not be used or allowed to delay the proceeding or to harass a member.

Chapter 11

Meetings

A meeting is the official assembly of the members of an organized group, club, society, or association or of any organized component of the group, such as a committee, commission, or council. The length of the meeting is measured from the time of convening to the time of adjournment.

In contrast, a convention (see Chapter 12) is usually a group of meetings taken in close succession over the course of one or more days. Customarily, the time between such meetings is considered a recess, with adjournment at the conclusion of the final meeting. Adjournment is usually sine die (without a day being set for the next meeting), denoting the finality of adjournment.

CONTINUED MEETINGS

If the assembly chooses to continue the meeting at a definite later time, it may do so. The subsequent meeting is legally a continuation of the original and action begins, after the establishment of a quorum, where it was interrupted at the time of adjournment. In a continued meeting, rules applicable to the original meeting still apply and matters pending at time of adjournment of the original meeting are still pending. Since a continued meeting is legally a continuation of the original meeting, special notice is not required, though a reminder to the members is helpful. One meeting can be continued any number of times. However, a continued meeting cannot be scheduled to coincide with the next regular meeting or at a time beyond the next regular meeting.

REGULAR MEETINGS

The bylaws of many organizations fix the times of the regular meetings, and since the membership is expected to be familiar with the bylaws, no official notification of such meetings is required. Other groups, without specific bylaw direction, customarily meet at previously agreed-upon times, and consequently no official notice is necessary. However, regardless of how the time of the meeting is set, it is courteous and beneficial to routinely notify the membership of approaching regular meetings.

If an organization has established, by rule or custom, a pattern of regular meetings at an appointed place, the time and place cannot be changed without notification to all members. No official action can be taken by the group prior to the stated time, or that set by custom, unless all members are present and consent.

A regular meeting cannot be convened unless a quorum is present, and once convened it follows the established order of business. In the absence of a quorum, those present may vote only to adjourn after fixing the time for the next meeting.

However, if a quorum is not present at the appointed time, rather than immediately adjourning the meeting it is sometimes helpful to hold a general discussion (totally informally and unofficially) of some of the main issues to ascertain the opinion of the group and the division among them. This is particularly helpful if some members have prepared material, have traveled a considerable distance, or have made special effort to be present and are anxious to speak to the group, even if reduced in size. Should a quorum develop and the meeting officially open (or even if action must await a later meeting) considerable time and future debate might be saved.

SPECIAL MEETINGS

A special meeting is one that is not regularly scheduled and is held to handle one or more specified matters of business. If the bylaws do not specify those authorized to call a special meeting, it is generally considered that the presiding officer, the executive committee, or a significant number of members can call one on proper notification. At a special meeting a quorum must be present, and if a majority disapproves of the called meeting it can be adjourned immediately.

Not only must all members be notified of an upcoming special meeting, but the notice must clearly state the item(s) of business that will be considered. Each item to be considered must be clearly stated and such general phrases as "old business" are not allowed. If action is to be taken at the meeting, this fact also must be stated in the notice.

Only items specifically stated in the notice of the meeting can be considered at a special meeting.

The item(s) of business to be considered at a special meeting should be listed in order in the notification to members, and this list constitutes the order of business for the special meeting. To document this order of business, a copy of the notification, or call, of the special meeting should be attached to the minutes of the meeting.

FAILURE TO CALL MEETINGS

When those empowered and authorized to call a meeting, generally the president, officers, or board of directors, fail to call it, any member or members may demand that a meeting be called. If action to call is still refused, the member(s), after a reasonable time, may call the meeting, notifying all concerned of the time and place (preferably the usual place). When a quorum is present, the meeting proceeds.

Responsibility of the Presiding Officer

PLANNING AND PREPARATION

Responsibility for a meeting usually lies with the presiding officer. This begins with planning and preparation for the meeting. It is the presiding officer's ultimate duty, often delegated to staff or to colleagues, to ensure that the physical aspects of the meeting area are accessible, comfortable, conducive to effective work, and such that all in the meeting area can follow the proceedings easily. For larger organizations, the site of the meeting may be decided by the membership, by the governing board, or by custom. Whatever the size of the membership, in scheduling meetings the convenience, the comfort of all, and easy access for at least a majority of the members must be considered.

It is the presiding officer's responsibility to see that the hall chosen for the meeting is of adequate size and has sufficient seating, lighting, amplification, and heating or cooling.

Any member, under question of privilege, can interrupt the proceedings at any time and state a request for more air conditioning in the back of the room, more seats for the alternate delegates, a microphone that works in one corner of the room, and so forth. It is the responsibility of the presiding officer to see that such requests are fulfilled so the assembly can function in comfort with maximum efficiency.

PROPER NOTIFICATION

The presiding officer also has the responsibility, if the time and site of the meeting are not well established, to ensure that the members of the group have been properly notified and that a time convenient to a majority of them has been chosen. It is the responsibility of the presiding officer to see that the meeting starts at the appointed time and concludes in a reasonable period. He or she must constantly keep in mind, from the opening gavel to adjournment, that he or she is in charge and responsible for the success of the meeting.

CONDUCT OF BUSINESS

The chair is not just another member who has the gavel at the moment. He or she is responsible for an orderly, productive, and expeditious session during which decisions will be reached. The chair who is well versed in parliamentary procedure, informed about the issues under consideration, and perceived as fair and equitable to all can lead the assembly to determine the will of the majority while protecting the rights of the minority. A good presiding officer, by virtue of his or her knowledge, tact, acceptance by the members, and, often, well-placed humor, can encourage the group to complete the business of the meeting as close to the appointed time as possible.

"WITHOUT OBJECTION"

The chair accomplishes this orderly conduct of business by sensing the will of the group, sometimes suggesting action that the group might want to take, by helping to phrase motions, and frequently by using that magical phrase "without objection." Noncontroversial issues often can be settled by stating that a certain action will be taken unless there is objection; and because so frequently there is no objection, considerable time is saved by not taking votes whose outcome is clearly predictable. The membership is totally protected since, on the objection of a single member, any issue that proves to be controversial must be put to a motion, a second, debate (if the matter is debatable), and a vote.

THE ART OF PRESIDING

A good presiding officer, in addition to being well grounded in parliamentary procedure and fully comprehending the potential ramifications of the issues being discussed, must also practice the art of presiding. He or she must be willing to make firm rulings. Such an individual is aware that much can be accomplished and time saved by using such rulings as "The motion appears to have been approved" and, if unchallenged, "The motion is approved," or by taking only a voice vote when one side of the issue appears clearly to dominate. Any member, unconvinced, immediately may request division of the assembly in such a case. That this is done only rarely emphasizes the confidence assemblies place in their presiding officers.

Proceedings are likely to become laborious and boring when the presiding officer follows the assembly rather than leading it. This is evidenced when a presiding officer, failing to sense that the assembly is anxious to move forward, allows debate to wander away from the issue and from reasonable time limits and insists on standing votes on questions which prove to be noncontroversial. Good presiding officers have no fear of being challenged by the membership; in fact, they encourage it whenever appropriate.

The Order of Business

Many organizations have their own order of business stated in bylaws or standing rules. If such an individual order has not been established, the following items, in order, should be considered at a meeting:

1. Call to order.
2. Disposition of minutes of the previous meeting(s).
3. Reports of officers.
4. Reports of boards, standing commissions, and standing committees.
5. Reports of special committees.
6. Unfinished business.

7. New business.
8. Announcements.
9. Adjournment.

An order of business is simply a standard outline of procedure for considering specific parts of the business of the meeting. Great flexibility should be allowed and encouraged. The chair may ask after the call to order if other agenda items are desired or if a variation from the order of business is preferred. If there is any controversy, he or she may ask that the specific agenda for the meeting be adopted or, more likely, announce that items have been added and the order of considering items changed to accommodate the members and, without objection, this new order will be followed.

If a member desires that his or her item of business be considered at a specific time, he or she may request this and, without objection or by a majority vote if there is objection, it may be allowed. The chair and members should not feel a loyalty to preserve the standard order of business unless they have a specific, justifiable reason.

CALL TO ORDER

The presiding officer should call the meeting to order promptly at the appointed time. Even in smaller, informal meetings, a call to order is helpful in getting all attention centered on the chair and eliminating casual conversation.

Examples

PRESIDING OFFICER: The meeting will please come to order.

PRESIDING OFFICER: The 140th Annual Meeting of the House of Delegates of the American Medical Association is now in session.

Often, the atmosphere of the entire meeting and the authority of the chair is set by the call to order. If it is done at the appointed time in an authoritative, confident voice, the members of the assembly immediately sense that it will be a businesslike, well-conducted meeting to accomplish the stated agenda and that the presiding officer is in charge. If the meeting is started late, in a lackadaisical, uncertain, or casual manner, the opposite impression is likely.

If there is to be an invocation or prayer, the chair announces it at this time and it is accomplished.

MINUTES OF PREVIOUS MEETINGS

The minutes of the previous meeting, or any meetings for which the minutes have not been considered, need to be approved. If the members have not had access to a copy of the minutes, the minutes are read, usually by the secretary, after which the chair asks if there are any additions, deletions, or corrections to the minutes as read. If there are changes, and these changes are accepted by the assembly, the presiding officer then asks for a motion to approve the minutes as amended. If there are differing opinions concerning the suggested changes, a vote is taken, the proper changes ascertained, and the minutes accordingly amended and adopted as amended. If there are no suggested changes, the chair asks for a motion to approve the minutes as read, and this is handled in the accustomed manner of a second, discussion, and vote.

When all members have received copies of the minutes prior to the meeting or the minutes are brief enough to be read rapidly by the members, the actual reading by the secretary may be dispensed with. Still, the presiding officer asks for corrections, additions, or deletions. Any changes are decided as above, and the presiding officer asks for a motion to approve the minutes as published or to approve the published minutes as amended. A simple majority of those voting gains approval of the minutes.

REPORTS OF OFFICERS

All officers who are required or who desire to make reports present them, usually in order of rank. Usually the president, the vice president, the secretary, and the treasurer report in this order.

After each report, questions and discussion are in order. If the report recommends action, a vote must be taken at this time. Usually the reporting officer will make a motion as part of his or her recommendation. After a second, further discussion ensues, and a vote is taken. If the report is purely informational, filing is proper, and the presiding officer accomplishes this quickly by stating, without objection, that the report will be filed. If there is objection to filing or a desire to take a different action, a specific motion, second, discussion, and vote must be taken.

Filing acknowledges that a report has been received and considered but that no action upon it is necessary or desirable. This does not have the effect of placing the organization on record as approving or accepting responsibility for any of the material in the report.

REPORTS OF BOARDS, COMMISSIONS, COMMITTEES

When there is a report from the board of directors or the executive committee, this report is given first (after the reports from officers). Reports from standing commissions or standing committees are then given, and action items are handled in a manner identical to action items recommended by officers. Action items which come from boards, commissions, or committees, when two or more members of these groups are members of the parent membership, come with an automatic second. The presiding officer can frequently expedite action by acknowledging the second rather than taking the time to ask for a second from the membership. If these reports are informational, they may be filed, without objection.

Special committee reports follow standing committees, and their reports are handled in an identical fashion. If any committee report is lengthy, it is advisable to have a written copy of the report in the hands of the members prior to the meeting and have the chair summarize the report and answer questions on it, rather than read the report to the members.

UNFINISHED BUSINESS

Unfinished business consists of business which was pending and not completed at the last meeting and also any matters which may have been postponed definitely to this particular meeting.

The chair introduces this order of business by announcing, "We will now consider unfinished business" or "Is there any unfinished business?" One of the duties of the presiding officer is to be aware of any unfinished business and to introduce such matters, if a member does not do so. After the members have been reminded of the unfinished topic, the secretary is called upon to read the motion and the usual second, discussion, and votes are entertained.

The fact that a subject may have been discussed previously does not make it unfinished business. Similarly, business that was postponed temporarily (tabled) or referred to a committee is not unfinished business. Business previously postponed temporarily is brought back for consideration by a successful motion to resume consideration (take from the table). Business previously referred to a committee is brought back to the assembly in the committee report.

NEW BUSINESS

The presiding officer then moves to new business by declaring, "New business is now in order" or asking, "Is there new business?"

At this time any member may propose any appropriate motion that he or she desires or may bring a matter for consideration before the group, even if action is not desired. Not infrequently, the presiding officer will have been asked by others or by an absent member to present an idea or suggestion to the group and will ask if anyone present wishes to make a motion concerning the matter.

The fact that an idea or suggestion is brought before the assembly does not mean that a motion must be made. If the members are not interested, the matter dies. If there is interest, a motion must be made and seconded before it can be discussed.

ANNOUNCEMENTS

The success of a meeting is enhanced by having a standard place in the order of business for announcements and by requiring that they be given only at that time. Reminders of the time and location of future meetings of the assembly or of upcoming meetings of the board of directors or of committees are also made during this period.

ADJOURNMENT

The presiding officer cannot declare a meeting adjourned, unless the lack of a quorum has developed. However, he or she may solicit such a motion by inquiring, "Is there a motion to adjourn?" If such a motion is then made, seconded, and carried, the presiding officer should formally announce the termination of the meeting, simply stating, "We stand adjourned."

Quorum

A quorum is the minimum number or proportion of the members of an organization that must be present for the valid transaction of business. As soon as the meeting is called to order, the presiding officer must be sure that a quorum is present and, if there is doubt, take a count. In the absence of a quorum, the only official actions that can be taken are to fix a time for the next meeting and to adjourn.

Every organization has the right to set its own quorum, and this number should be stated in the bylaws. If the organization does not have an established quorum, parliamentary law fixes the quorum as a majority of the members.

A majority may be unduly restrictive, especially for large groups; in such a case the group chooses a more realistic number. Ideally, the required number should be small enough to ensure that a quorum usually will be present and yet large enough to prevent a small minority of members making decisions for the entire group.

Organizations with a fixed number of members usually choose a definite number as a quorum, while those with a fluctuating number of members tend to select a percentage as a quorum. However, great latitude is available, and some organizations determine that those members attending a meeting will constitute a quorum. If such variations are chosen, they must be stated as options in the bylaws.

A meeting of a board or a committee requires the majority of its members for a quorum.

A mass meeting or an organization without a definite membership uses the number of persons present as a quorum.

In a convention to which official delegates are sent, a quorum is always the majority of the qualified delegates unless otherwise stated in the bylaws.

A quorum always refers to the number of members present at the time of a vote, not to the number voting. If a quorum is present, and since abstention from voting is allowed, there may be a vote in which the number of votes cast is smaller than the quorum.

COUNTING THE QUORUM

Only members in good standing are counted in computing a quorum. Organizations may define "in good standing" in any way they choose in their bylaws, often not extending the privilege of voting to associate members, affiliate members, or delinquent members.

Any member in good standing may disqualify himself or herself or be disqualified because of conflict of interest in a particular question. Such individuals are not counted in computing the quorum. The presiding officer is a member of the organization and is counted in determining a quorum.

All members in good standing have the right to vote; they also have the right not to exercise that privilege.

THE VANISHING QUORUM

Though the presence of a quorum is established at the beginning of the meeting, with the coming and going of members the quorum may disappear. Consequently, any member is justified, through parliamentary inquiry, in asking the presiding officer if a quorum is present. The presence of the proper number will be ascertained by either a head count or a roll call. If the absence of a quorum is suspected and a vote is taken, a request for a count must be made immediately after the vote. A later suggestion that a quorum may not have been present when an earlier vote was taken has no validity. Similarly, the request for the establishment of a quorum cannot be used repeatedly as a means of delay. Having established the presence of a quorum and in the absence of an obvious egress of a significant number of members, the chair may rule any further request for a count to be out of order.

Debate

Deliberative groups accomplish their work by decisions made after thorough consideration and debate on proposals submitted to them. The equal right of every member to debate any proposal is a basic principle of parliamentary law. To maintain this equity, debate is controlled by parliamentary rules, and every member should be familiar with these rules in order to participate most effectively.

Requests and some motions are not debatable, specifically the motions to adjourn, to postpone tem-

porarily, to vote immediately, to resume consideration, to suspend the rules, and to consider informally.

The main motion and the motions to amend, to rescind, and to appeal are fully debatable.

All other motions are debatable, but debate is limited to specific points.

GAINING RECOGNITION

A member must gain recognition by the presiding officer before beginning his or her debate. This is done
in various ways, according to the size of the meeting.
In a very small meeting a raised finger or a nod of the
head to the chair may indicate the desire to speak. In
a somewhat larger group the member rises from his
or her chair, addresses the presiding officer, and
waits for recognition. In a large meeting where microphones are available, it is permissible for the
member to approach the microphone and wait until
recognized by the chair.

The proposer of a motion or a committee member
who has presented a report is customarily given the
first opportunity for debate, particularly to explain
the motion or report.

Members who have spoken once on an issue
should wait until all others desiring to speak have
done so before requesting a second opportunity.

RULES OF DEBATE

Debate should be restricted to the immediately pending matter. For example, if debate is on an amendment to the motion, it should be limited to the
amendment and not to the motion itself.

Debate must be relevant. If a speaker departs from
the immediately pending issue, it is the responsibility
of the presiding officer to ask him or her to please restrict comments to the matter under consideration.
Any member who feels that the speaker is not addressing the issue at hand may rise to a point of order
and call the attention of the chair to the digression.
The chair, if he or she agrees, then requests the
speaker to limit his or her remarks to the pending
question.

Proper parliamentary conduct prevents a member
from using dilatory tactics to confuse an issue or delay proceedings. It is the presiding officer's responsibility to ensure that such tactics are not used. If it ap-

pears that obfuscation or delay is intended, the chair should immediately remind the speaker that this is unacceptable and, if necessary, rule the action out of order.

ROLE OF PRESIDING OFFICER

Discussion is always addressed to the presiding officer, never to another member, and it must be done in a courteous and orderly manner. The chair should never allow a verbal attack on another member or his or her motives and should not allow the assembly to become inattentive, noisy, or disruptive. It is the presiding officer's responsibility to maintain order and courtesy at all times. It is also his or her duty to see that only the immediately pending issue is being discussed and that parliamentary rules are being followed.

If the assembly has placed a limit on debate, it is the chair's responsibility to enforce this limit, and he or she can use any means, such as an official timer, for assistance. In a limited debate, time allocated to one member cannot be transferred to another.

Just as irrelevant and unlimited debate should not be allowed, the chair should also be very cautious at all times to avoid the appearance of cutting off debate. However, when it appears that all who desired to speak have spoken, the chair expedites the work of the assembly by asking, "Is there further debate?" or stating, "Seeing no other discussants, let us vote immediately." Again, the members are protected in that any member who wants to speak and has been unrecognized may obtain the floor by rising and stating a desire to speak anytime before the outcome of the vote is announced.

INFORMAL DISCUSSION

Sometimes it is beneficial to have informal discussion of a matter before a formal motion is proposed. At other times, after a motion has been made, discussion can be more meaningful and expeditious if it is done informally rather than by adhering strictly to parliamentary rules. In either instance, informed discussion can be accomplished by the incidental motion to consider informally. After such a discussion a vote is taken; this vote automatically terminates the period of informal discussion.

The informal method of debate is particularly helpful when a problem presents without an obvious solution. For example, a member may rise and point out that the organization is in dire need of more members though he or she has no specific method to suggest for obtaining them, and he or she might then move to consider informally the problem of membership. If the motion is successful, an informal discussion ensues, followed by a motion which terminates the period of informal discussion, and the rules of debate and voting on the motion then follow the established method.

This often very helpful method of debate has previously been known as committee of the whole, in which the entire assembly acts as a committee.

THE MAJORITY VOTE

Making decisions by a majority vote (more than half of the votes cast) is a basic principle of democracy as expressed through parliamentary procedure. As a general rule, fewer than a majority should not be authorized to make a decision, and more than a majority vote (such as by plurality) or a requirement of more than a majority vote (such as two-thirds) must be specified in the law, in the bylaws, or in the organization's adopted rules of procedure.

The larger the number of votes required, the less control and protection the majority has, since as the number required increases, the size of the minority to prevent the action decreases. The extreme is the requirement of a unanimous vote, as a minority of one can prevent the vast majority from having its desires served.

Special exceptions to the principle of requiring only a majority vote are made for motions that would restrict or significantly change the rights of every member. Such motions are those to vote immediately (prevent further discussion), to limit debate, and to suspend the rules.

As a general rule, it is inadvisable to require more than a majority vote to decide the assembly's wishes.

WHAT IS A MAJORITY?

Since "majority" can mean any number of things, the term should be clearly defined in the organization's bylaws or the assembly's rules of operation. There are five principal ways in which a majority may be defined accurately: majority of all delegates, majority of all qualified delegates, majority of delegates present, majority of a quorum, and majority of legal votes cast.

As an example, in the deliberative assembly (House of Delegates) of an association there are, say, 400 delegates, each of whom is authorized to attend the meeting and to vote. However, only 390 have qualified by having their credentials certified (found to be in good standing), and 380 are actually present. If the bylaws of the association require only 100 delegates as a quorum but only 50 vote on a specific issue, a majority vote would vary as follows:

Majority of all delegates	201
Majority of qualified delegates	196
Majority of delegates present	191
Majority of a quorum	51
Majority of legal votes cast	26

Majority vote of all delegates. For the example we are using, this definition would be inappropriate, but for a small group with a fixed membership it is appropriate and frequently used. It simply means a vote of one more than half of all delegates to the meeting, whether they are present or absent.

Majority vote of all qualified delegates (in good standing). This means a vote of more than half of all the delegates, present or absent, but certain members may be excluded (not in good standing) for some reason (nonpayment of dues, noncertification, and so on). With a large group, such as the House of Delegates in our example, this majority might impose a hardship, in that the 10 who are not in good standing still count as part of the quorum but do not count in the voting.

Majority vote of delegates present. The failure of some delegates or members to vote does not reduce the number of affirmative votes needed for passage, which is one more than half the number of delegates at the meeting. Consequently, an abstention serves as a negative vote.

Majority of a quorum. A majority of a quorum for a large group could also be small. In our example, the quorum is established at 100, so only 51 affirmative votes could make a decision for the entire group of 400.

Majority of legal votes cast. This definition is most commonly specified, and it is the one used if majority is not clearly defined. Thus, unless the bylaws or the adopted rules of order define a majority to be another number, a majority vote means one more than half the number of legal votes cast.

The principle of majority rule, based on a majority of those voting (a quorum being present), derives from the fact that every member has the right to vote. Those who waive this right accept the vote of the majority. Since they cannot be presumed to have voted either affirmatively or negatively, literally they have not voted.

TIE VOTE

A tie vote on a motion means that the same number of votes have been cast in the affirmative and in the negative. Since a majority (more than half of the legal votes cast) is required to pass a motion, the motion fails. In such a case, the chair, if he or she is a member of the organization and has not already cast a vote, may vote to break the tie or even make a tie. He or she has the right, as does every member, to elect not to vote.

A tie vote in an election or on two or more alternative propositions in which the candidates or the propositions all receive an identical number of votes constitutes a deadlock. No action has been taken. Such a dilemma is resolved by continuing to retake the vote until a change occurs or until the assembly accepts another method of voting.

PLURALITY VOTE

A plurality vote is a vote of at least one more than the number received by any opposing candidate or issue. A plurality vote is applicable only when there are three or more candidates or alternative issues. For plurality voting to be used, the bylaws or the rules of procedure of the association must clearly specify its use. In this instance, a majority is not necessary.

As an example, under a plurality vote when 100 ballots have been cast the results could be as follows:

Candidate	Vote
A	42
B	41
C	17

Candidate A is the winner under plurality voting, but if his or her ideology is markedly different from those of candidates B and C, the wishes of the majority have not been served. Under majority voting, there would be no election and another ballot would be taken.

UNANIMOUS VOTE

A unanimous vote is one in which all legal votes cast are on the same side of the issue or for the same candidate.

The term *unanimous vote* can be qualified in many ways. For example, if a board requires a unanimous vote of all members, it means whether the members are present or not. A unanimous vote of those present is clearly different from a requirement for a unanimous vote of all those present and voting.

The requirement of a unanimous vote is discouraged because it gives tremendous power to a minority. It is seldom used.

TWO-THIRDS VOTE

A required two-thirds vote, used in controlling debate, suspending the rules, and voting immediately, has the same problem of definition and is subject to the same definitions as are majority votes. When it is undefined, it refers to two-thirds of the legal votes cast.

A rapid way of determining whether a vote has passed by two-thirds is to double the number of negative votes cast and compare it with the number of affirmative votes. For example, of 100 legal ballots cast, if 69 are affirmative and 31 are negative, the motion carries since 69 exceeds twice the number of negative votes (62).

A MAJORITY OF SEPARATE ELECTIONS, QUESTIONS

When more than one question or more than one office is being voted on, the number of votes on each question or office is computed separately. Since all eligible voters may not vote on each question or each race, each stands on its own number of votes cast, a majority of that number being required for approval or for election.

A MAJORITY IN GROUP ELECTIONS

When there are several candidates running for several offices of equal rank, the assembly has two methods of authorizing elections.

In the first, all candidates compete with each other for one of several positions of equal rank. For example, if there are twelve members running for three at-large positions on the board of trustees, to be elected a candiate must do both of the following:

1. Receive a majority vote of the total number of legal ballots cast for all of the positions.
2. Receive a vote that is ranked within the number of offices to be filled (in this case three).

Both requirements must be met. For example, if 100 members vote and each member makes 3 choices (300 total votes cast), the count might be as follows:

Candidate	Vote
A	65
B	60
C	55
D	53
E	51
F	16

All candidates except the last received a majority (51) or more, but since there were only three positions open, only candidates A, B, and C were elected. Candidates D and E, even though having obtained a majority, are not elected.

The second method of determining a majority when electing a group is by the slotting method. Those eligible to run for each slotted seat are determined geographically, numerically, or by other means. Candidates A and B may be competing for the first vacancy, for instance, candidates C and D for the second vacant seat, and candidates E and F for the third vacant seat. Rather than competing against the entire field, only two candidates are competing in each race. In many instances a highly qualified candidate may be defeated (by being matched with another highly qualified candidate) while a less-qualified candidate is elected (by being matched against another poorly qualified candidate).

This method can be used in instances where the terms of the vacant seats vary. For instance, all candidates can compete against each other, with the understanding that the one who gets the most votes will get the seat with the longest term, and the second highest vote getter will take the seat with the lesser tenure. An alternative is to have an agreement that the top vote getter will receive the longest term, after which another vote will be taken of all the other candidates and then the highest vote getter will receive the remaining, shorter-term seat.

CAN THE PRESIDING OFFICER VOTE?

No one can be disenfranchised by being elected to office. The presiding officer has the same right as every other member to vote (though not to propose motions or nominate candidates), but customarily the chair does not exercise his or her right to vote, except when that vote is by ballot or when one vote could alter the outcome. By not voting on individual issues unless there is a tie vote, the chair greatly enhances the perception of his or her impartiality.

When the voting is by ballot, the presiding officer (if a member of the organization) has the same right as everyone else and is free to exercise this right.

NO ONE REQUIRED TO VOTE

No member of the assembly, including the presiding officer, can be required to vote. On a ballot vote, any member, including the presiding officer, can submit a blank ballot if it is important not to be perceived as having abstained.

CONFLICT OF INTEREST

It is an excellent principle that any member should not vote on an issue in which he or she (or his or her immediate family or business partner) has a direct personal interest, financial or otherwise, that might appear to be served by a particular vote. It is often beneficial that such a member announce publicly that he or she is abstaining, an action that can be entered into the minutes if it is thought to be important.

Exceptions are corporations in which stockholders can vote and the large number voting obviates an individual conflict, or organizations voting to fix the compensation of its members. Were such voting not allowed, it would be impossible for the compensation to be set by the group.

With issues involving the entire organization, when more than one member will be equally affected, every member has the right to vote. As an example, if the assembly is voting to establish compensation or travel expense reimbursement for delegates to a meeting, this can be voted on by the delegates because everyone is affected.

If an organization brings charges against a member, that individual cannot vote on the charges. However, if more than one member is named in the charge, all are allowed to vote. This is done to thwart the possibility of a minority group of members bringing charges against a majority of the members.

METHODS OF VOTING

In a democratic society the right to vote is a basic, sacred right. In an assembly every member has the right to vote on every issue and in every election. Likewise, every member has the right not to vote. In a vote by ballot, any effort to have votes disclosed, such as a motion to have the election by ballot declared unanimous (possibly forcing members to vote against the motion), is illegal.

When the bylaws of the organization do not prescribe how voting should be done, the method can be determined by a motion and a majority vote at any time before the vote is taken.

The most frequently used methods of voting are

1. By general consent
2. By voice vote
3. By raised hands
4. By standing vote
5. By roll call
6. By ballot
7. By mail

The chair normally decides how the vote will be taken, but on special occasions a member may desire to make a motion to have the assembly choose the method. The presiding officer usually chooses the method that he or she feels is most expeditious and accurate.

For noncontroversial issues, voting by general consent is a great help, and the chair's use of the term "without objection" is extremely helpful. Any member who objects simply states the objection, and a vote is taken in the usual manner. A voice vote is most frequently used. If the presiding officer is in doubt, he or she may call for a show of hands, and if there is still doubt a standing vote is taken. Usually the outcome is evident, but if there is persistent doubt, tellers are used to accurately count each number.

VOTING BY GENERAL CONSENT

Voting by general consent is sometimes called "by unanimous consent," and a wise presiding officer uses it frequently to expedite business. He or she may propose action and, after a pause continue by saying, "Without objection, this will be done," or by asking, "Is there objection?," pause, and, hearing none, continue, "Without objection it is accomplished."

The rights of the members are protected under this method because at any time any member may object and require a vote. This objection may be expressed even after the presiding officer has announced that an action has been taken by general consent, but the objection must be made immediately thereafter.

The method of general consent is not to be used for any controversial issue, but it is very helpful in accomplishing the routine actions of a meeting, such as approving the minutes, receiving announcements, granting privilege of the floor for announcements, and approving the monthly reports.

VOICE VOTE

The voice vote (*viva voce*) is the commonly used method of deciding most questions. This allows the vote to be determined rapidly but is not accurate on close counts. It is possible for a loud minority to outshout a quieter majority, and when there is doubt the chair asks for a show of hands, which often clearly demonstrates the outcome of the vote. Failing this, the chair asks for a standing vote, and if the outcome is still not evident, a count by tellers is performed.

SHOW OF HANDS

If the chair senses that the vote will be close, he or she may originally call for a show of hands. If the outcome of a voice vote is indefinite, or if any member has asked for division of assembly, the chair may then ask for a vote by raised hands. Having all members raise the same hand makes it easier to ascertain and count the numbers. Consequently, the presiding officer may say, "All in favor of the motion please raise their right hand. . . . Now lower your hands." If the difference between the ayes and the nays is clearly visible, the result is evident. If it is still in doubt, the chair then asks the tellers to count the raised hands, which accounts for the need to ask those voting to keep their hands raised until the tellers have completed the vote and then have the entire group lower their hands simultaneously. Otherwise, in a large assembly, those tellers with the largest number of votes to count may not reach a certain row until after a member has lowered his or her hand in the belief that the vote has been concluded.

STANDING VOTE

Voting by a standing vote is frequently used when a voice vote or show of hands leaves the count undecided. It is also the preferential method on a controversial issue when a two-thirds vote is required.

The chair should clearly outline the issue being voted on and then give instructions:

PRESIDING OFFICER: Those voting affirmatively please stand and remain standing.

PRESIDING OFFICER (after determining that the tellers have completed this part of their work): Will those standing now please be seated. Will those opposed to the motion now please stand and remain standing.

PRESIDING OFFICER (on completion of the tally): Will you please resume your seats?

Even when a two-thirds vote is required, such as for adoption of a bylaw change, if the subject appears not to be controversial, the chair is correct in first asking for a voice vote. If there are no (or a very few) negative votes, he or she then announces, "The motion has passed by a two-thirds vote." This frequently saves time when it is apparent that the two-thirds vote was accomplished, but this method is always subject to a vote by raised hands or a standing vote, if any member requests division of the assembly.

ROLL CALL

Voting by roll call is time-consuming and laborious, but it is sometimes advantageous when delegates want to have a record of their vote to carry back to their constituents. It is sometimes called a vote by ayes and nays and may be required by the bylaws for voting on certain matters. If it is not required, any member may move to have a roll call vote. This is not a request and is handled in the usual fashion for motions, requiring a majority vote. This motion is subject to misuse by some who hope to delay the proceedings or embarrass others by public record of their vote, but the assembly always has the option of voting the motion down if it appears that its motivation is improper. The roll call vote itself is taken after the presiding officer clearly explains the motion and announces:

> **PRESIDING OFFICER:** We will move to the roll call vote. . . . Those in favor of the motion will vote Aye as their names are called, those opposed will vote No, and the votes will be recorded by the secretary.

The order of the roll call vote is usually alphabetical, but it may be by areas of representation or by any manner the assembly determines. The secretary should repeat each member's vote after it is cast to ensure accuracy.

VOTING BY BALLOT

Voting by ballot is usually required in elections. The bylaws may require that some matters be determined by ballot voting. This method can be very useful in deciding emotionally charged, highly controversial issues. Any member can propose this method by making a motion, which is nondebatable and non-amendable, and the assembly can decide quickly if this is its method of choice.

It behooves the presiding officer and the officers of the association, if an election is expected or if highly controversial issues are anticipated, to ensure that all preparations have been made to take a ballot vote without delay. The presiding officer should instruct the delegates on how voting will take place, remind them that defaced or confused ballots will be excluded, and ensure that every member has a ballot and that all have been turned in before the tellers leave the room.

VOTING BY MAIL

Voting by mail can be done only if it is authorized in the bylaws of the organization. When authorized, it requires a specific motion and a majority vote to be implemented.

The disadvantage of voting by mail versus voting by informed delegates after full discussion is obvious. However, at times an assembly may run out of time, feel that its delegates are well informed, and vote to have a mail ballot.

Some organizations with a widely dispersed membership may choose to use mail ballots for elections and for decisions on important issues. In such instances, every effort should be made to have had nominations open to the membership and to ascertain that all members receive information on the issues they are being asked to vote upon.

Unless the bylaws provide for a particular plan, a ballot containing the names of those facing election or information about proposed measures or amendments, together with full instructions from the elections committee, is sent to each member. The ballot must be marked and returned to the secretary within a specified time period. The question of preserving secrecy is perhaps best addressed by having the ballot returned in a plain sealed envelope within a second envelope which contains the member's name. The secretary receives the letter, records that the member has voted, and then sends only the plain envelope containing the ballot to the elections committee.

One distinct disadvantage of mail balloting is that there may be a very poor return of ballots and consequently the decision or choices may be made by a small minority. This can be prevented by a bylaws requirement that decisions by mail are valid only if a majority of a quorum of the members return ballots.

VOTING BY PROXY

The use of proxies in an organization in which all members have an equal vote is not advised and is seldom used. It is never permissible unless authorized in the public statutes or in the organization's charter or bylaws. This method, which allows one member to give written authorization to another member to vote in his or her place, is useful in the corporate structure but is not compatible with the basic rights of members in a membership association.

VOTING RESULTS

It is the responsibility of the presiding officer to announce the results of every vote, regardless of how it is taken. Even in a voice vote when the outcome is apparent, the presiding officer should announce, "The motion is carried" or "The motion fails." This protects the right of a member who may not have been in a position to clearly hear the vote, and it assists the secretary and other recorders of the meeting to know exactly what the chair has ruled. However, an inaccurate announcement by the chair does not legally change the vote as it was recorded.

CHANGING A VOTE

A member may change his or her vote when it was taken by a show of hands, by rising, or by roll call, up until the time that the result is announced. On a vote by roll call a member may change a vote after the announcement only by proof that an error was made in recording his or her vote. On a ballot vote, a member may not change his or her ballot once that ballot has been delivered to the tellers or placed in the ballot box.

ALL VOTES ARE BINDING

To anticipate a formal vote, an assembly may be tempted to take a straw ballot or an informal vote to see how many members favor the motion in principle or how many favor the sense of the motion. It is sometimes felt that if one side of the division might be shown to have a stronger position, the ultimate voting might be more favorable to that side.

All such efforts are illegal. Every vote taken in a meeting is binding upon that assembly. It cannot take a nonbinding vote. If the members of the assembly are agreeable, a recess can be taken whereby the strengths and weaknesses of the issue might be determined informally in the hallways. Any vote taken in the meeting is binding.

Chapter 12

Conventions

A convention is usually a group of meetings taken in close succession over the course of one or several days. Though every member of an organization is entitled to attend its convention, most groups find it advisable, and larger organizations find it necessary, to delegate the authority to establish policy for the organization to a smaller legislative body such as a house of delegates. The parent body has the responsibility of determining the qualifications for delegates to its legislative group and of deciding how large the legislative body should be and how representation in it is apportioned, but it is the local (the represented) group that determines which individual(s) should represent it.

Once elected and convened, the elective group has full authority for setting the policy of the organization, and it is the responsibility of the elected officials and the employed staff to implement these policies. This assembly elects its own officers (speaker, vice speaker, and so on) and carries out other duties given it by the constitution and bylaws, including electing the officers of the organization (in some instances trustees, major councils, and committees as well), establishing the length of terms of office, and in effect controlling the operation of the association. In other instances, the organization will retain for the entire membership the right to elect major officials by mail ballots, cumbersome as this sometimes may be in a large association.

Delegates

Once elected by a constituency, each delegate should feel that he or she represents the entire membership of the association and should strive always to make decisions and to vote for what is best for the entire group, keeping in mind the desires and convictions of his or her constituents. Usually, the local groups meet with the delegates, review the upcoming agenda, and discuss the major issues to be faced at the convention. The local constituent group may

113

feel that it wants to instruct its delegates how to vote on certain issues. Unless a particular issue is of truly outstanding importance to the local group (such as a resolution they are proposing), it is always best that delegates attend the convention well informed as to the feelings of their constituents but not instructed by their colleagues at home. It should be realized that the delegates, once assembled, will hear many viewpoints expressed, be exposed to perhaps new information and strong contrary opinions, and can make the best decision and be most effective by voting their conviction at the time of the vote.

OFFICIAL CALL

An official call to all delegates is made well in advance of the convention, usually by the president, speaker of the house of delegates, secretary-treasurer, or other appropriate officer. The call should clearly state where and when the meeting will be held, provide a list of the delegates and alternate delegates who will be seated, and give the names of those who will serve on the major convention committees and reference committees. These lists are useful as delegates may want to converse with other delegates or members of the major committees about matters particularly important to them. Likewise, as much of the agenda as is available—resolutions, reports, resource documents, and so forth—should be sent to all who are expected to attend the meeting, early enough for them to become thoroughly familiar with the materials prior to the convention. Later-developing aspects of the agenda are made available to the delegates at the time of their arrival at the convention site or as soon as they become available. It is the responsibility and obligation of the speaker, officers, and staff to spare no effort to have all information that will be useful to the convention in the hands of the delegates at the earliest possible moment. Only a thoroughly informed assembly can do its work intelligently and expeditiously.

Convention Committees

The number, type, and size of convention committees varies with the size of the organization, its function, its method of operation, and its agenda. Common to most legislative bodies are a credentials committee, a committee on rules (rules and order of business), and a committee of tellers (with a designated chief teller). There may be a bylaws committee, a program committee, and other committees appropriate to the particular organization. These committees are frequently collectively called *convention committees,* as they have specific duties related to the conduct of the convention; *reference committees* handle the substance of the convention agenda, that is, the reports and resolutions which the assembly must consider and make decisions on.

CREDENTIALS COMMITTEE

The credentials committee usually consists of three to five members who examine the credentials of the delegates and certify the delegates to the speaker. Though much of the routine work can be handled by staff, this committee is not infrequently called upon to settle disputes about whether a delegate has met the association's requirements or between contesting members for a particular seat. As an example, a delegate may feel that his or her term has not expired, but the president, the executive committee, or others have appointed a new delegate to be seated. The credentials committee will gather information and, if the matter is still unresolved, will make recommendations to the house of delegates, which may be required to make the final decision on which individual is seated.

The credentials committee is also responsible for certifying to the speaker as the assembly begins its work that a quorum of properly certified delegates is present. Anytime later in the meeting, if the credentials of a delegate are questioned or a question arises about the seating of a delegate, this committee may again be called into session.

RULES COMMITTEE
(RULES AND ORDER OF BUSINESS)

The rules to be followed by the assembly are likewise recommended by a convention committee. Smaller assemblies may simply have a rules committee; larger organizations refer to it as the rules and order of business committee. This committee presents to the assembly, at the beginning of its initial session, a recommended set of rules which will be followed during the convention, any unique rules which are thought advisable for the particular session (such as added security or limitation of debate), the time and place of elections (if any), and the order of business. Many organizations, particularly larger ones, might already have published the proposed order of business in the information sent out before the convention, and the assembly simply adopts this or a modification of it. Once this report is adopted by the assembly, any deviation from it must be approved by a majority of the delegates.

Some organizations set a deadline for receiving resolutions so that the resolutions may be distributed to the delegates in the preconvention packet. Such organizations may use the committee on rules and order of business to study any late resolutions, interview the proposers, and recommend to the assembly whether or not certain resolutions should be accepted. Ordinarily, if the proposing organization, for good reasons, could not meet the deadline or if the resolution relates to an issue which developed too late for a routine resolution to have been written, the committee may recommend that the late resolution be accepted. The final decision to accept or to reject a proposed late resolution must be made by the assembly.

TELLERS

Every large assembly finds that although most issues are decided by a voice vote, it is often necessary to take a vote by show of hands, by standing, or even by ballot. At times, the difference between the ayes and the nays is apparent when the hands are raised or the delegates stand, but if there is any question a count must be taken.

An adequate number of tellers must have been appointed and instructed (even rehearsed) as to which area of the hall each will count and how to report their findings to the chief teller. A large number of delegates can be accurately counted in a very short time by experienced tellers.

Should voting by ballot be necessary, the tellers have the responsibility to see that the written ballot is received only by official delegates (when others may be seated with delegates), is properly handled and returned, and that the tally is accurately taken and reported to the presiding officer.

BYLAWS COMMITTEE

If the association does not have a standing committee or council on constitution and bylaws, it may appoint a bylaws committee. This group has the responsibility to continually review the constitution and bylaws in view of changes in circumstances and current actions of the assembly, to review proposed amendments to the constitution or bylaws, and to make recommendations to the assembly for any action thought necessary. The committee has the obligation to forward any proposed changes, even though it may recommend against their adoption.

Approval of recommended changes in the constitution and bylaws requires only a majority vote of the assembly even though the organization may have a stricter requirement (such as a two-thirds vote) to actually adopt the changes. A vote on approval of recommended changes gives the assembly an opportunity to decide whether or not it wants to even consider a proposed change.

The committee on rules (or the committee/council on constitution and bylaws), following such a favorable action by the assembly, then has the responsibility of putting into proper language the proposed changes and resubmitting the matter to the assembly for adoption or rejection. In those organizations that require more than a simple majority vote for adoption, the required number is mandatory.

PROGRAM COMMITTEE

Though larger associations will have the program of the entire convention planned and publicized months ahead of the convention, smaller groups may find a program committee very useful. This group also needs to plan well ahead of the time of the meeting. It has the responsibility to schedule the meetings, activities, special events, and social events, working closely with the president and other officers. The program committee submits its recommended program for the convention at the opening session; once it is adopted, changes in the program are the responsibility of the assembly itself.

Reference Committees

Unlike convention committees, which work on the details of the convention, reference committees handle the agenda of the legislative body itself via reports and resolutions.

A reference committee is expected to hold hearings on every item of its assigned agenda in one half or one full day, hold its executive session, and prepare its report that evening. If the work assigned to the committee appears to exceed this expectation, some of the items should be assigned to another reference committee. Each committee usually consists of three to five members of the assembly appointed by the presiding officer. They act as agents of the assembly to study issues referred to them and to make recommendations to the parent body.

Reference committees permit an assembly to very thoroughly study and make decisions on an amazingly large agenda. As the volume of work of the assembly increases, additional reference committees permit it to handle an ever-enlarging agenda in the same brief period of time, without losing the thoroughness of its investigations and the quality of its decisions.

Smaller organizations may use standing committees as reference committees during the convention, or they may appoint two or more reference committees to consider general areas such as finances, matters intrinsic to the organization, and matters extrinsic to the association. Larger organizations will tend to assign one category of business to a specific reference committee. Medical associations, for example, may have one committee that considers only the reports from its board of trustees, another that considers legislation, another on medical education, another on hospitals and medical facilities, another on scientific and public health, and one on amendments to constitution and bylaws (which replaces the rules committee of smaller groups). Also useful are miscellaneous reference committees, to which are assigned matters that do not fall directly into the established categories. By the use of such reference committees, an association with 450 to 500 delegates can properly and thoroughly handle an agenda of more than 300 individual items in a standard two-and-one-half- to three-and-one-half-day business session.

Reference committee hearings are open to all members of the organization, delegate or not, to official observers from other organizations, to guests, to interested outsiders, and to the press if approved by the assembly. Any member of the organization, delegate or not, is privileged to speak on any and all matters under consideration by the reference committee. Nonmembers, guests, or interested outsiders may, upon recognition by the committee chair, be permitted to speak. The chair may call upon anyone attending the hearing if, in his or her opinion, the individual may have information which would be helpful to the committee.

As with any meeting, the responsibility for seeing that the hall is adequate in size, that it has sufficient seating, proper lighting, and temperature control, and that the proceedings are equitable and fair rests with the chair. This person also has jurisdiction over such matters as photography, television filming, and the use of recording devices. If, in his or her estimation, such activities would be, or would become, undesirable for the conduct of an orderly hearing, he or she may prohibit them.

The reference committee may establish its own rules on order of business, limitation of time for each speaker, and all ground rules. Though this is a mixed meeting of members, nonmembers, and even some who have only limited interest in the proceedings, all courtesies expected in a democratic meeting should be adhered to.

Though the members of the reference committee are in effect judges as well as hearing officers, they may participate in the questioning of those testifying to make sure that they understand the opinions being expressed, or they may answer questions if a member seeks clarification. However, the committee members must be vigilant to avoid expressing opinions during the hearing, asking questions that might betray a bias, or entering into an argument with the speakers. The reference committee chair should be very careful not to ask for an expression of collective sentiment on any issue or to attempt to take an informal vote or straw ballot.

The reference committee hearing is the proper forum for the discussion of controversial items of business. Ideally, most of the necessary debate on issues will be presented in the reference committees and not repeated in the meeting of the house of delegates.

Reference committees publicize the order in which items coming before them will be considered so delegates can plan their appearances. In spite of this, the concurrent time of reference committee hearings may create difficulties for a delegate who needs to testify in two committees at the same time. By prior notice and arrangement, the reference committee chair will often allow testimony out of normal order when such a conflict occurs. Also, the presiding officer of the assembly is usually very tolerant in allowing debate on the issue, as brought up by the reference committee's report, realizing that even the best-intentioned delegate may not have been able to give his or her testimony earlier.

Following its open hearing, the members of the reference committee go into executive session for deliberation, debate among themselves, and construction of their report. The committee has the right and the obligation to call into such executive session any individual or any data which it feels might help it in reaching a conclusion. Other than for such invited guests, the reference committee executive session is closed.

Minority reports from reference committees are in order.

REFERENCE COMMITTEE REPORTS

The quality of the work of a deliberative body which uses the reference committee system and the expeditious fashion in which it operates are directly dependent on the quality of the reference committee reports. Since the substance of these reports constitutes the bulk of the official business of the assembly, how well they are constructed, how clearly they can be interpreted, and how unbiased they are in their presentation determine the pace and the efficiency of the assembly when it convenes to consider them. Consequently, no effort should be spared to make them clear, succinct, and accurate.

The reports need to be written as quickly as is feasible after the completion of the executive session so that they can be processed and made available to the delegates as far in advance of their formal presentation as possible. The organization is well advised to assign senior, experienced staff to the reference committees to facilitate the writing, checking, editing, and rewriting of the reports. Customarily, members of the reference committee return, often very late at night, to review and approve the final draft, which goes to the assembly over their signatures.

The reports, if properly prepared, have been carefully screened to ensure that the committee is expressing exactly what it desires to say in the most succinct and correct form, that no unnecessary legal problems or areas of confusion are going to be raised by the report, and that ambiguities have been removed so that the delegates will clearly understand what is intended and the debate will be on the substance and not on the form of the report.

The members of the committee, in coming to their conclusions, use all available facts, data, and the testimony that has been presented to them. The number of speakers in the reference committee hearing does not necessarily influence their opinion. A single individual testifying before the reference committee can be more persuasive, and in the minds of the members of the committee more correct, than any number of speakers presenting the opposite view. Just as there are no straw ballots during the hearing, the committee should not be influenced by the number who spoke on one side or the other but should truly limit their conclusions to the substance of the issue.

The committee may amend resolutions, accept one resolution in lieu of a kindred but different resolution, consolidate similar resolutions, or propose a substitute resolution that expresses its recommendation. It may recommend the usual parliamentary procedures for disposition of the business before it, such as adoption, rejection, amendment, referred for report, referred for decision, and the like.

At the time the reference committee report is presented, each report and each resolution which has been accepted by the assembly as its business must be acknowledged, but it is the recommendation of the reference committee concerning the substance of these specific reports or resolutions that is the pending issue.

It is recommended that each item referred to a reference committee be reported as follows:

1. Identify the resolution(s) or report(s) by number, title, and sponsor.
2. State concisely the committee's recommendations.
3. Comment, as appropriate, on the testimony presented at the hearings and on any other data used by the committee in reaching its conclusions.
4. Incorporate supporting evidence for the recommendations of the committee.

In addition, the committee may or may not choose to use a consent calendar as a part of its report. Wherever appropriate, it is strongly recommended that the consent calendar be used to expedite the workings of the assembly, eliminate unnecessary verbiage and formality, and save the time of the members.

CONSENT CALENDAR

The consent calendar or waiver of debate list includes those items referred to the reference committee which are of a noncontroversial (though possibly very important) or informational nature or which generated little or no debate during the hearings. These items are listed at the end of the reference committee report with the committee's recommendation for adoption, rejection, or referral attached to each. For convenience and ease of handling, the items on the consent calendar are grouped according to the recommendation. Each item carries a number (following the numbered items in the main report) and the title of the resolution or report. A sample consent calendar follows.

CONSENT CALENDAR

Recommended for Adoption:
(19) Resolution 167: Quality of Care and Proposed Medicare Cutbacks
(20) Resolution 195: Coverage of Drugs by Medicaid
(21) Resolution 247: Employed Physicians

Recommended for Referral for Report:
(22) Report RR of Board of Trustees: Financing

Long-term Care and Catastrophic Health Insurance

(23) Resolution 195: Coverage of Drugs by Medicaid

Recommended for Referral for Decision:

(24) Resolution 215: Congressional Record

Recommended Not for Adoption:

(25) Resolution 113: Cost of Legal Services

(26) Resolution 170: Medicaid Disproportionate Share Fund for Physicians

Recommended for Filing:

(27) Board of Trustees Report LLL: Report of the Special Task Force on Professional Liability

When the consent calendar is presented, the presiding officer will allow time and remind members that they have the right to extract any item they wish. Any member wishing to debate or even to call attention to an individual item requests extraction without the need for a vote on permission to separate it from the other items. When all items that members desire to extract have been removed, the remaining items are considered as a package. Following this, the extracted items are individually considered. Items dealing with amendments to the bylaws should not be placed on the consent calendar if, as is usual, the bylaws require more than a majority vote to be amended.

REAFFIRMATION CONSENT CALENDAR

Associations that have been meeting and establishing policy for years or decades often find that members offer resolutions proposing what is already association policy. Such members may be unaware that such policy has been established or may want to emphasize the matter. To prevent the assembly's having to receive the resolution, refer it to a reference committee, and act again on it in the full assembly, such resolutions can be placed on a reaffirmation consent calendar. This group of resolutions is then handled as soon as the assembly begins officially to receive resolutions (usually at the first session).

The presiding officer will remind the members of their right to extract resolutions, the few extracted ones will be referred to a reference committee (along with all other resolutions), and the remainder are adopted as a group.

This method saves a great deal of time and effort and does not interfere with the rights of the members, as any resolutions can be extracted and referred upon request.

HANDLING THE REFERENCE COMMITTEE'S RECOMMENDATIONS

On each item in the reference committee report, the action recommended by the committee can be handled in either of two different ways:

1. The recommendation is phrased as a motion—that is, to adopt, to not adopt, to refer for report, to refer for decision, and so forth. The motion is made as soon as the reference committee chair reads that part of the report to the assembly. Discussion, debate, and further action proceed from this point.

2. The recommendation is phrased not as a motion but simply as a recommendation. The chair then opens the matter for discussion, without a motion having been made. The effect is to permit full consideration of the business at hand, unrestricted to any specific motion for its disposal. Any appropriate motion for amendment or disposition may be made from the floor. In the absence of such a motion, the chair will state the question in accordance with the recommendation from the reference committee and a vote is taken. This method allows the assembly to begin and direct the discussion wherever it chooses. If it chooses to follow the recommendation of the reference committee, whether or not there has been discussion, time is saved by the chair's stating the question and taking the vote rather than asking for a motion and a second.

The second method might be used to expedite the work of the assembly in several ways, five examples of which follow.

- The reference committee is reporting on informational material which encompasses no specific proposal for action. The reference committee expresses appreciation for the information and recommends that the matter be filed for information. The chair declares the matter to be before the assembly for discussion. When there is no discussion and no motion proposed, the chair may declare, "It is filed" or "Without objection it is filed," without the necessity of a formal vote. Such a statement records the action and concludes this item of business.

- The reference committee is reporting on a resolution which it believes should be rejected, and it so recommends. The chair places the resolution before the assembly for discussion. In the absence of a motion from the floor, the chair, at the appropriate time, places the question on adoption of the resolution, emphasizing that the reference committee has recommended a vote in the negative. It should be clear that the vote is on the resolution, not on the reference committee report.

- The reference committee is reporting on a resolution which it feels should be transmitted for further consideration to the board of trustees or through the board to an appropriate committee, and it so recommends. The chair places the matter before the assembly for discussion. It may be that the assembly prefers to adopt this matter, amend it, refer it for decision, postpone it, or table it, any one of which it is free to do; or the assembly may wish to follow the reference committee's recommendation. If there is no motion from the floor, the chair puts the motion on the recommendation of the reference committee to refer. If this fails to pass, the motion is then on adoption of the resolution.

- The matter placed before the assembly for discussion is the amended version of a resolution as presented by the reference committee together with a recommendation, not a motion, for its adoption. It is then in order for the assembly to apply to the reference committee version amendments of the first and second degree in the usual fashion. Such procedure is orderly and does not preclude the possibility that a member may wish to restore the matter to its original, unamended form. Such restoration may be accomplished simply, since it may be moved to amend the reference committee version by restoring the original language.

- The reference committee is reporting on two or more kindred resolutions and it wishes to recommend a consolidation into a single resolution, or it wishes to recommend adoption of one of these items in lieu of the other. For orderly handling, the matter before the assembly for consideration is the recommendation of the reference committee for the substitute or consolidated version. A motion to adopt this substitute is a main motion and is so treated. If the reference committee's version is not adopted, the entire group of proposals has been rejected, but it is in order for any member to then propose consideration and adoption of any one or several of the original matters.

IMPORTANCE OF PARLIAMENTARY LANGUAGE

There has been some confusion and lack of understanding regarding the language used in handling the business of an assembly. This has been especially true of such motions as those to approve, to accept, to adopt, to endorse, to refer for report, to refer for decision, and the like.

In the interest of clarity, the following explanations are offered.

1. When the assembly wishes to acknowledge that a report has been received and considered, but that no action upon it is necessary or desirable, the appropriate proposal for action is that the report be "filed." For example, a report which explains a government program or regulations or clarifies the issues in a controversial matter may properly be filed for information. This does not have the effect of placing the organization on record as approving or accepting responsibility for any of the material in the report.

2. When a report offers recommendations for action, these recommendations may be adopted, approved, or accepted, each of which has the effect of making the organization responsible

for the matter. Language such as "accepted for information," "approve in principle," or "favor the sense of the motion" should be avoided.

3. The term "endorse" expresses definite approval, implying a commitment to implementation.

4. If the assembly does not wish to assume responsibility for the recommendations of a report in their existing form, it may take action to refer back to committee (recommit), to refer to other groups, to reject the report in its entirety or in specific part, or to adopt as amended (amend and adopt).

5. The assembly should take definite action on all resolutions submitted to it and only if necessary reaffirm current policy. If no action is the only appropriate posture for the assembly on a particular resolution, the reference committee may choose to place this resolution on the consent calendar in the category designated "no action." If adopted, the motion to take no action fulfills the obligation of the assembly to act on every piece of business submitted to it, and it quashes the resolution for the current meeting. The presiding officer can expedite this procedure by stating, "Your reference committee has recommended no action. Without objection, no action will be taken."

Chapter 13

Nominations and Elections

A nomination is a formal presentation to an assembly of the name of a member as candidate for an office to be filled. There are numerous ways in which nominations might be made legally, the three most usual being

Nominations from the floor
Nominations by committee
Nominations by petition

The bylaws of the organization should clearly state the offices to be filled by election, the eligibility and required qualifications of candidates, the method and time of nominating, and the term of each office to be filled. If nominations are to be made by committee or by petition, the bylaws should elucidate how this will be carried out, the responsibilities of those who will oversee the process, how the committee will be determined or how the petition will be received, and how the reporting from either method will be done.

The bylaws should state the method of nominating officers, but if they do not, any member may offer a motion specifying how nominations are going to be accrued and presented, or the presiding officer may choose a method and, "without objection," implement it.

NOMINATIONS FROM THE FLOOR

In small or moderate-sized organizations, nominating from the floor is the easiest method, and it is usually quite adequate. At the time of the announced election, the presiding officer starts at the top of the slate to be elected and asks for nominations, in turn, for each of the offices to be filled. After one, two, or more candidates are nominated, the presiding officer pauses, asks if there are other nominations, and, if there are none, moves on to the next office to be filled. Should there be no nominations, the presiding officer may ask the group, "How does the assembly wish to proceed with nomination?" or "Do you desire a nominating committee be appointed to present nominations?"

In larger assemblies, nomination by committee is usually essential to selecting the best-qualified candidates and securing their commitment to serve, but even when nominations are presented from a committee, further nominations from the floor are in order unless specifically prohibited in the bylaws.

Nominations do not require seconds. Much confusion exists concerning this; rarely an unnecessary and embarrassing situation arises when there appears to be no one anxious to second a nomination. The confusion persists, perhaps because many organizations allow endorsing statements, which are known as "seconding speeches." If the report of the nominating committee states the qualifications of its nominees, a nominator from the floor has an equal right to state the qualifications of his or her proposed candidate.

The presiding officer must be extremely careful to avoid the perception of rushing nominations or attempting to prevent, by haste, a nomination. Consequently, he or she should not only repeat the request for further nominations but also allow adequate time for these to be made. When no other nominations are made, the presiding officer may declare the nominations closed or simply move on to the next office for which nominations are to be made.

A formal motion to close nominations is not required, but in larger assemblies where the chair may not be well known to or a close friend of all members, he or she is well advised to ask for such a motion or to declare that nominations are closed and pause before proceeding. Even after nominations have been closed, they may be reopened by motion until voting has actually begun.

For any organization, no matter how small and informal, to rely solely on spontaneous nominations from the floor is dangerous. A small committee or a single individual recruited to solicit nominations results in a more substantive list of candidates. Such an individual or small group, just like a formally appointed nominating committee, must seriously consider all eligible candidates. At times it may be necessary to encourage some member to accept the nomination. An assurance by the nominee that he or she is willing and able to serve is required.

NOMINATIONS BY COMMITTEE

A nominating committee is an extremely important part of any organization, and it should be carefully selected. It should consist of thoughtful, industrious, well-informed, and experienced members of the organization who are representative of the entire membership. Nominees should represent not only the major aspects of the organization's interest and work but also its diversity of gender, geography, background, and ideology. To attempt to achieve this representation, some organizations elect the members of the nominating committee on a geographic basis, by areas or districts, and the bylaws may stipulate how age groups, gender, minority groups, or experience in the organization are to be represented. Some groups, seeking experience and dedication to the association's ideology, require recent incumbents to serve, as, "The membership committee shall consist of the five most recent past presidents of our association." Again, the bylaws should protect the membership by allowing nominations from the floor in addition to those from the committee.

THE NOMINATING COMMITTEE

Once selected, the members of the nominating committee should take their duties extremely seriously, realizing that the future of the association depends on continued leadership. Members should accept their responsibility only if they have the commitment, the time, and the willingness to do a thorough job. No member should think this is a perfunctory duty, easily accomplished or serving a primarily honorary function, as "We have several senior members who should be so honored." Nomination to high office, while indeed honorable, invariably carries grave responsibilities. The committee must truly study every office and all possible candidates for it, consult potential nominees, if necessary convince the individual of the need for him or her to serve at this time, and to report in a timely fashion with pride and conviction that the best possible candidates have been selected.

The bylaws of the organization should clearly state the duties of each office and the qualifications of those selected to fill each office.

Members who aspire to serve in one of the offices for which nominations will be made should decline a position on the nominating committee. However, members of the committee cannot be disqualified from nomination because of their service on the committee. Not infrequently, as the nominating process continues, thorough investigation and discussion may reveal that perhaps the best candidate is a member of the committee. Once the committee has made the decision to nominate one of its members, that member should resign from the committee.

Whether there should be a single slate (one nominee per office) or a multiple slate (at least two nominees for each office) is a continuing problem for many organizations.

Proponents of the single-slate philosophy believe that the very best candidate should be identified and nominated, with the membership being protected by an opportunity to make nominations from the floor. Many highly qualified members will accept such a nomination, realizing that other nominations are unlikely, but are not willing to subject themselves to competition with a fellow member and a campaign for election. Consequently, some organizations that require a multiple slate lose the service of some very good members.

Proponents of the multiple-slate system believe it is more democratic to have contested races and refer to the fact that we have a two-party political system nationally. But this system vastly increases the difficulties encountered by the nominating committee. If the committee decides that a single individual is the best possible candidate and pits him or her against the next best-qualified candidate, it runs a great risk of losing the services of one, since defeated candidates often are reluctant to run again. The alternative is to pair a fully qualified candidate with a candidate of lesser qualifications in the hope that the former will be elected.

Consistently, more and more nongovernment groups are moving to the single-slate method of nomination, with the belief that they thus have the opportunity to present the best-qualified candidate for each office and that if they do not achieve this, the membership will correct it by nominations from the floor, or even by write-in ballot.

No action is taken on the report of a nominating committee; the nominations are accepted just as if they have been made from the floor.

NOMINATION BY PETITION

Nomination by petition, now much less used than formerly, was at one time particularly favored by large organizations with many relatively small units. In the case of nomination by petition, the bylaws provide that petitions bearing a specific number of signatures (usually not too large a number to discourage usage) sponsoring a candidate are acceptable if received by a specific time prior to the election. Organizations using this method usually provide standardized forms. Any petition judged to be in order results in the candidate's name being placed in nomination as if nominated from the floor. If this method is to be used, the bylaws must be specific and detailed concerning the requirements to be met.

NOMINATION TO MORE THAN ONE OFFICE

Offices within an organization are termed compatible or incompatible, the latter denoting a conflict of interest between the duties of two offices. Some groups combine compatible offices such as secretary and treasurer. The bylaws of an association may allow officers such as the president and president-elect to serve as members of the governing board, thereby emphasizing the compatibility of these positions.

No member can accept nomination for or hold two incompatible offices. A member nominated for two such offices at the same election must accept nomination for only one.

Unless prohibited in the bylaws, an officeholder may be a candidate for another office. If he or she is elected to and accepts an incompatible office, the former position is vacated.

Elections

The bylaws of the organization should contain specific information concerning the time, place, and method of voting, the method of conducting the election, a statement of who is eligible to vote, the vote necessary to elect, the time when newly elected officers take office, and a provision to fill vacancies.

The formality and complexity of the elective process varies with the size of the organization. Small groups may accept a show of hands or a written ballot using a blank sheet of paper. However, for even the smallest group, proper procedure must be followed, and if a secret ballot is required or requested, it must be provided.

Moderate-sized organizations frequently appoint an election committee, which actually conducts the election. This group is entrusted with providing the necessary material (including printed ballots, if advisable), distributing ballots to members at the meeting (or by mail, if allowed), and collecting and tallying the ballots. This group prepares a report of the results of the election.

Large organizations usually provide an elective process in their bylaws. Most commonly, a printed ballot is prepared following the conclusion of nominations and a secret ballot is held at a clearly and previously announced time. The management of the election and the tallying of the vote are the responsibility of tellers, under the supervision of trusted senior officials or staff members who work with the process repeatedly. The tellers verify each ballot as to accuracy and compatibility with the bylaw requirements, tally the vote, and submit to the presiding officer an official election report.

RULES OF ELECTIONS

If the organization's bylaws do not clearly state the rules of elections, these rules should be followed:

1. Qualified members may be voted for, even though they have not been nominated. A write-in vote is legal.
2. A mistake in voting for the candidates in one category (such as an excessive number of votes) invalidates that portion of the ballot but no other portions.
3. A torn or defaced ballot is valid if the intent of the voter is clear and the intent is valid.
4. A technical error, such as misspelling, does not invalidate a ballot if the voter's intent is clear.
5. Blank ballots or write-in votes for unqualified persons are counted as ballots cast but as illegal ballots.

6. If several nominees for equal office (such as a board of trustees), are voted for in a group, a ballot containing fewer votes than the number of positions to be filled is valid unless prohibited by the bylaws. A ballot containing a vote for more than the number of positions to be filled is illegal for all the positions, and this portion of the ballot becomes invalid. If other portions are in order, they are still valid.
7. If the total number of ballots cast exceeds the number of eligible voters, the vote must be retaken.

REPORT OF THE TALLY

The tellers or the election committee should submit a written report, concurred in by all members of the committee, to the presiding officer and containing the following information:

Number of qualified voters:
Number of legal ballots cast:
Number of illegal ballots rejected:

Contest A

Candidate	Vote
1	
2	
3	

Contest B

Candidate	Vote
1	
2	
3	

Contest C

Candidate	Vote
1	
2	
3	

All tellers, or all members of the election committee participating in the election and tally, sign the election report, thereby certifying its accuracy.

UNCONTESTED NOMINEES

At the time of formal nominations, if there is only one candidate for a specific office, it is customary for the assembly, after adequate time for other nominations has been taken, to elect that nominee by voice vote. This is usually handled by the presiding officer, who says, after due delay for other nominations, "Seeing no other nominators, may I have a motion that nominations be closed and Ms. Smith be elected as our president-elect?" or "As there is only one nomination for the office of president-elect, all those in favor of electing Ms. Smith please say Aye. . . . Those opposed, No. . . . Ms. Smith has been elected as president-elect." This method replaces the antiquated system of having the office included on the ballot or having the ballot cast by the secretary when there is a single nomination.

CHALLENGES TO ELECTION

If a challenge to an election is to be made, it must take place during the election or in a reasonably brief time thereafter. If the reasons for challenging the election appear to be plausible—for instance, that ineligible persons have voted, that there was negligence in conducting the election, or that the elective process did not follow bylaw requirements—an investigation is usually made by the governing body or a group designated by it, or in any manner satisfactory to the assembly. A challenge of one member to the right of another member to vote should be made to the credentials committee or to the tellers (or election committee) before the voting begins. The committee conducting the hearing then reports its recommendation to the assembly, which will make the ultimate judgment.

ELECTION RESULTS ARE FINAL

Barring any challenges, the vote as certified by the tellers or the election committee and announced by the presiding officer is final. The motion to change the vote to make it unanimous is usually well intentioned as a complimentary gesture, but it is not in order and cannot change the legal vote as announced.

ELECTED TERMS

In larger organizations the bylaws clearly state when newly elected officers should take office, such as at the conclusion of the annual meeting or at the beginning of the new year. If the bylaws do not speak to the time a tenure begins, elections are effective as soon as completed.

VOTING

In voting, members are not limited to those who have been nominated, either from the floor or by the committee, if the vote is taken by ballot or by roll call. Legal votes may be cast for any eligible member by writing in that name on the ballot or by verbal expression on roll call. Thus, any member receiving the necessary vote is elected, whether nominated or not.

VOTE NECESSARY TO ELECT

The vote necessary to elect should be clearly stated in the bylaws. If not, the following rules control.

1. The candidate receiving a majority of the legal votes cast for a single office is elected.
2. Unless the bylaws provide for election by plurality, a candidate receiving a plurality of legal votes cast, but not a majority, is not elected.
3. If a majority of votes is required for election and this is obtained by no candidate, the requirement for a majority vote cannot be waived. The assembly must adopt a procedure which would allow the election to be completed, for instance by dropping the candidate receiving the lowest number of votes after each ballot.

Parliamentary Terms Defined

Adhere To be attached to or dependent on. Pending amendments adhere to the motion to which they are applied.

Ad hoc committee A committee that completes a specific task and then is discharged.

Adjourn To officially end a meeting.

Adjourned meeting A meeting that is a resumption at a specified time of an earlier regular or special meeting. The adjourned meeting is legally a part of the original meeting. Same as *continued meeting.*

Adjournment sine die (without day) The final adjournment ending a convention or a series of meetings.

Adopt To approve by vote and give effect to a motion or a report.

Affirmative vote The total yes or aye vote supporting a motion.

Agenda The official list of items of business of a meeting or convention.

Amend To change a motion.

Apply A motion is said to apply to another motion when it may be used to affect the first motion.

Assembly A meeting of the members of a deliberative body.

Ballot vote The expression by ballot, voting machine, or otherwise of a choice with respect to any election or vote taken on any matter as a secret ballot.

Bylaws The set of rules adopted by an organization defining its structure and governing its functions.

Call of a meeting The written announcement distributed to members prior to a meeting indicating the time and place of the meeting and stating the business there to be brought.

Chair The presiding officer of a deliberative body.

Challenging a vote Objecting to a vote on the grounds that one or more voters does not have the right to vote.

Challenging an election Objecting to an election on the grounds that it was not conducted properly.

Close debate *See* Vote immediately.

Consent calendar A section of a report or of an organization's agenda including matters which are expected to be approved without discussion and without dissent. Any member desiring to discuss or oppose an item may have that item removed from the consent calendar and considered by the assembly.

Continued meeting *See* Adjourned meeting.

Convene To open a meeting or convention.

Cumulative voting The casting of more than one vote for a candidate when several offices are to be filled, instead of voting for as many candidates as there are vacancies.

Debate Formal discussion of a motion or proposal by members under the rules of parliamentary law.

Delegation of authority An assignment of authority by one person or group to others to act in their stead.

Dilatory Tactics Misuse of procedures or debate to delay or prevent progress in a meeting.

Disposition of a motion Action taken on a motion to implement its purpose.

Division of the assembly A request for a show of hands or a standing vote.

Division of the question A request calling for separation of a motion into two or more parts, each to be discussed and voted on independently.

En bloc As a group.

Ex officio member One who is a member of a committee or board by virtue of holding a particular office.

Executive session Any meeting of a committee or organization which is attended only by members unless others are requested by the body to attend.

138

Floor A member "has the floor" when he or she receives formal recognition from the presiding officer and is thus the only member entitled to speak or to make a motion.

General consent An informal method of approving routine motions by assuming unanimous approval unless objection is raised. Also known as *unanimous consent*.

Germane amendment Amendment relating directly to the subject of the motion to which it is applied.

Hearing A meeting of an authorized group for the purpose of listening to the views of members or others on a particular subject.

Illegal ballot A ballot that does not conform to the rules governing ballot voting; thus, it cannot be counted.

Immediately pending question The last proposed of several pending motions and therefore the one open for immediate consideration.

Incidental motion A motion without precedence that deals with a procedural question arising incidentally from the pending motion. Examples are motions to appeal, to suspend rules, and to consider informally.

Informal consideration Consideration and discussion of a matter or motion without the usual restrictions on debate.

In order Permissible and correct from a parliamentary standpoint at a particular time.

Main motion A motion which brings business before the assembly.

Majority A number that is more than half of any given total.

Majority rule Rule by decision of the majority of those who actually vote.

Majority vote More than half the number of legal votes cast for a particular motion or candidate, unless a different basis for determining the majority is required.

Meeting An official assembly of the members of an organization or of any organized component of the group, such as a committee, commission, or council. The length of the meeting is from the time of convening to the time of adjournment.

Member in good standing Any person who has fulfilled the requirements for membership in an organization and who has not resigned, been suspended, or been expelled from membership.

Minority A number that is less than half of any given total.

Minutes The official record of the actions of a deliberative body.

Motion A proposal submitted to an assembly for its consideration and decision.

Multiple slate A list of proposed candidates containing the names of more than one nominee for each office.

Nomination The formal proposal to an assembly of a person as a candidate for an office.

Out of order Not correct, from a parliamentary standpoint, at the particular time.

Parliamentary authority The text or system of parliamentary procedure adopted by an organization.

Pending question Any motion that has been proposed and stated to the assembly for consideration and that is awaiting decision by vote.

Plurality vote A larger vote than that received by any opposing candidate or by an alternative proposal.

Point of order The raising of a question as to the propriety of some action taken by the chair or by a member.

Precedence The rank of priority of a motion.

Preferential ballot A ballot on which the voter indicates more than one choice and the order of preference, so that subsequent choices can be taken into consideration without another election being needed because of failure of any candidate (or proposal) to obtain a majority on the first ballot.

Previous question *See* Vote immediately.

Privileged motion A motion not related to the pending business but of such urgency that it is given high precedence. Privileged motions include the motions to recess and to adjourn.

Proxy A signed statement authorizing a person to cast the vote of the person signing it. Proxy may also refer to the person who casts the vote.

Putting the question   The statement by the presiding officer of a motion to the assembly for the purpose of taking the vote on it.

Qualified motion   A motion that is limited or modified in some way in its effect by additional words or provisions. For example, "I move we recess at two o'clock for thirty minutes."

Question   Any proposal submitted to an assembly for decision.

Quorum   The number or proportion of members that must be present at a meeting of an organization to enable it to act legally on business.

Reaffirmation consent calendar   The group of resolutions which reaffirm existing policy. Any one can be extracted and referred to a reference committee.

Recall   A motion whose purpose is to undo a motion to refer.

Recess   A brief interruption of a meeting.

Recognition   Formal acknowledgment by the presiding officer of a particular member, giving that member the sole right to speak.

Renew a motion   To present again a motion previously lost at the same meeting or convention.

Request   The expression of the parliamentary rights of all members. There are two types. *Conditional requests* are those which may be granted by the chair or voted by the assembly. *Mandatory requests* are those that must be granted by the chair.

Rescind   To repeal a motion which has been passed.

Resolution   A formal motion, usually in writing and introduced by the word "Resolved," that is presented to an assembly for decision.

Restricted debate   Debate in which discussion is restricted to a few specified points of a motion.

Ruling   Any pronouncement of the presiding officer that relates to the procedure of the assembly.

Second   To endorse a motion proposed by another member so that discussion or voting may begin.

Seriatim Consideration by sections or paragraphs.

Single slate A list of proposed candidates containing the name of only one candidate for each office.

Special committee *See* Ad hoc committee.

Special meeting A meeting held at a time other than that at which the organization normally meets, called to handle one or more specific matters which are noted in the call to the meeting.

Specific main motion A main motion so frequently used that is has acquired a specific name to differentiate it from the general main motion. The most frequently used specific main motions are those to reconsider, to rescind, and to resume consideration.

Standing Committee A committee that has a specific area of responsibility and a fixed term of office.

Subsidiary motion A motion which changes the main motion or the manner in which it is handled. Subsidiary motions include the motions to amend, to refer for report, to refer for decision, to postpone definitely, to limit debate, to vote immediately, and to postpone temporarily.

Substitute motion An amendment that offers a new motion on the same subject as an alternative to the original motion.

Suspension of the rules A vote to disregard temporarily a rule that prevents the assembly from taking a particular action.

Table To set a motion aside until the assembly decides to resume consideration of it (to postpone temporarily).

Teller A member appointed to help conduct an election and help count the votes.

Term of office The duration of service for which a member is elected or appointed to an office.

Tie vote A vote in which the affirmative and negative votes are equal on a motion, or a vote in an election in which two or more candidates receive the same number of votes.

Unanimous consent   The adoption of a motion or procedural step (such as approving minutes) without a vote. If a member objects, a vote must be taken.

Unanimous vote   A vote without any dissenting vote.

Unfinished business   Any business that was pending and interrupted by adjournment of a previous meeting or was earlier postponed definitely to this meeting.

Voice vote   A vote taken by calling for ayes and nays and judged by volume of voice response.

Vote immediately   A motion which, if passed, ends discussion and mandates a vote. Earlier known as call the question or close debate.

Waiver of notice   Relinquishing of the right to be notified of a proposal or meeting.

Write-in vote   A vote for someone who has not been nominated, cast by writing the name of the person on the ballot.

Questions and Answers About Parliamentary Procedure

The following questions are often asked about proper parliamentary procedure. They are discussed in greater detail in the text but are placed here for easy reference.

Q: If the basic rule is that only one motion can be pending at a time, how can we keep making more motions?

A: The rule is that only one *main* motion can be pending at a time. Other motions, such as those to amend, to refer, and to postpone, directly relate to the pending main motion.

Q: When do actions resulting from a successful motion and the results of an election become effective?

A: Such actions and results are effective immediately unless the motion or the bylaws provide otherwise.

The successful motion might state that a dues increase will become effective at the beginning of the calendar year. If a time is not stated, the action is effective immediately.

The same is true for elections. Some bylaws specify that newly elected officers will take office at the end of the annual meeting or at the beginning of the fiscal year. In the absence of such a requirement, the newly elected persons take office immediately, even though a ceremonial installation may be scheduled later.

Q: Is it in order to move to vote immediately on all pending issues, or must action be taken individually on each of the pending issues?

A: Yes, it is in order to make such a motion if each pending item has been discussed. The chair should make special efforts to ensure that members clearly understand the motion.

Q: Is a hostile amendment in order?

A: Yes, if it is germane to the subject of the motion, even if it changes completely the intent of the motion. For example, a motion that the assembly condemn the president for calling monthly meetings of the organization can be changed by amendment to substitute the word "commend" for the word "condemn." This is germane to the motion, which is to express the assembly's opinion of monthly meetings.

An amendment that simply changes an affirmative statement of a motion to a negative statement is not in order. For example, a motion that the organization increase the dues by $25 per year cannot be amended by adding the word "not" before the word "increase." This simply reverses the order of the affirmative and negative votes. All motions should be positive statements.

Q: Must the motion to reconsider be made by a member who voted for the original motion?

A: No. The motion to reconsider can be made by any member regardless of how he or she voted on the motion itself.

Q: Does the motion to reconsider open the main motion to debate?

A: No, discussion on the motion to reconsider is limited to the reasons for reconsideration. Antiquated parliamentary procedure did allow the motion to be debated, but this is no longer acceptable.

Q: Does the motion to postpone temporarily (to table) ordinarily require a majority for passage but a two-thirds majority for passage if the motion is being used to dispose of a motion without debate?

A: No. Some parliamentary authorities have recommended such a difference, dependent on the intent of the proposer of the motion. However, it is clear that the presiding officer cannot always discern the motive or intent in the mind of the proposer and fairly make this judgment. Consequently, the majority should prevail. If the majority later feels that the matter should be considered or that it originally made an error in postponing the motion, the majority can vote to resume consideration (take from the table), so the membership is protected.

Q: When several members seek the floor, how does the presiding officer determine which one to recognize?

A: When a motion has been proposed, the proposer should be recognized first, if he or she seeks the floor, to allow an explanation of the reasons for the motion. After that, the first person to stand and address the chair should be recognized first. In large meetings and conventions using multiple floor microphones, the presiding officer actually keeps a tally on the order in which members appear before the microphone to await their turn, to be fair in recognizing them.

Q: What is a continued meeting?

A: If the assembly chooses to continue the meeting (instead of adjourning) at a definite later time, it may do so as a continued meeting. This meeting is legally a continuation of the original meeting and action begins, after the establishment of a quorum, where the original meeting was interrupted. Continued meetings can be continued any number of times. This was originally referred to as an adjourned meeting by some.

Q: In the absence of a quorum, what can be done?

A: Legally, those present may vote only to adjourn after fixing the time for the next meeting. However, it is sometimes helpful to have a general discussion (totally informally and unofficially) of some of the main issues to ascertain the opinion of the group and the division among them. This is particularly true if some members have prepared material, have traveled considerable distances to be present, and are anxious to speak to the group. Should a quorum develop and the meeting can officially be opened (or even if action must await a later meeting), considerable time and future debate might be saved.

Q: What is a vanishing quorum?

A: Though a quorum may have been present at the opening of the meeting, with the coming and going of members the quorum may disappear. Any member is justified, through parliamentary inquiry, in asking the presiding officer whether a quorum is present, especially before an important vote. If this is not done and the absence of a quorum is suspected, a request for a count must be made immediately after the vote. A suggestion that a quorum may not have been present when an earlier vote was taken has no legal validity.

Q: Must a proposed amendment be acceptable to the maker of the motion?

A: If the motion has not been stated by the presiding officer, it is still being developed and its maker may accept or reject any proposed changes to it.

   Once the motion has been stated by the chair, the motion is the property of the assembly and the assembly must decide whether and how the motion will be changed. However, considerable time can often be saved, if the proposed amendment is noncontroversial and appears to improve the motion, by the chair stating that without objection the amendment is approved. If there is objection, a vote must be taken.

Q: Is it proper for the proposer of a motion to speak or vote against it?

A: Yes. The proposer may have wanted to hear the subject discussed and during the discussion, or because of amendments adhered to the motion, may change his or her mind. No member in good standing should be denied the right to speak or to vote.

Q: Why would an assembly want to informally consider a matter and how is this done?

A: There are times when an assembly desires, or urgently needs, to develop a position and there is not sufficient time to refer the matter to a committee and await its report. Informal consideration allows the group to do its best, collective work in a brief period without the restrictions of parliamentary rules. This is accomplished by the passage of the incidental motion to consider informally. The pending motion is considered with the presiding officer recognizing those who wish to speak. This discussion is continued until the members decide to vote, and the vote terminates the informal consideration. Should no agreement be reached during the informal consideration, a motion is needed to terminate informal consideration.

This is a vast improvement over the antiquated and cumbersome method of the assembly resolving itself into a committee of the whole. That procedure required that the presiding officer turn the chair over to a temporary committee chair and that all votes be only committee votes not binding on the assembly. Voting had to be repeated after the committee voted itself back into an assembly with the original presiding officer again in the chair and after the committee chair had reported to the assembly the actions of the committee.

Q: Can an amendment be amended? Is it worth the confusion?

A: An amendment can be amended, but only once. This right is very important, and if the procedure is understood there should be little or no confusion. An assembly always takes one thing at a time. In discussing and voting on matters, it takes the most recently proposed and works back to the original. If there is a motion with a primary amendment and also a secondary amendment, discussion and voting must be on the secondary amendment, then on the primary amendment, and finally on the motion itself (as amended, if either the primary or secondary amendment is successful).

Duties of the Presiding Officer

To be successful, the presiding officer must remember the following things.

1. The ultimate responsibility for the success of the meeting is yours. The location, hall, seating, lights, amplification, and heating or cooling must be conducive to good attendance and effective participation.

2. The meeting should start on time and finish as close to designated adjournment time as feasible.

3. You maintain control of the meeting at all times and see that it is orderly and productive and moves expeditiously.

4. Every member of the assembly should be fully informed at all times, especially prior to a vote.

5. Every member who wishes to speak must have the opportunity to do so but must not abuse the opportunity by prolonged or repetitive speaking.

6. All remarks of members are made to the chair and not to other members.

7. You must explain the basis of every upcoming vote if necessary.

8. You must announce the results of every action or vote.

9. You can use the phrase "without objection" to quickly pass noncontroversial items.

10. You must be courteous and helpful to every member at all times.

11. You can break the monotony of the meeting periodically with humor, when and where appropriate.

12. Above all else, you must always be perceived as fair and equitable to all.

Duties of a Member of an Assembly

To be successful, every member of an assembly must remember the following.

1. Being selected as a delegate to an assembly is an honor that carries with it the responsibility of full attendance, participation, and reporting back to your constituency.

2. Every other member of the assembly deserves your respect and cooperation.

3. When you wish to speak, stand, approach the microphone (if one is being used), and wait for recognition.

4. When recognized by the presiding officer, state your motion or give your discussion.

5. After making a motion, wait until another member seconds the motion.

6. Listen carefully as the presiding officer states the motion, to ensure its accuracy.

7. If your motion is debatable, the presiding officer will allow you to begin the debate.

8. Always address your remarks to the presiding officer, even when you are answering another member's question.

9. Never verbally attack another member or use abusive language.

10. If you believe the presiding officer has erred in a ruling, appeal the ruling of the chair and have the assembly decide.

11. If you believe that there has been a violation of the rules, an omission, or an error in the proceedings, rise to a point of order and request a ruling from the presiding officer.

12. If you are unclear about the pending motion, for example whether it is debatable or amendable, or if you need help in correctly wording your own motion, rise to parliamentary inquiry. The presiding officer will answer your inquiry or offer you help.

13. If you are unclear about the outcome of a vote or doubt the accuracy of the announced result, request division of the assembly and have a tally.

Index

For Additional Copies of
Rules of Order by James E. Davis, M.D.

Check your local bookstore or use this form.

Name _____

Address _____
(No P.O. Box)

City _____ State _____ Zip _____

Phone _____

	Price	×	Quantity		Total
Rules of Order	$24.95	×	_____	$	_____
Shipping and handling, first book ordered	$ 3.00	×	1	+	3.00
Shipping and handling, each additional book	$ .50	×	_____	+	_____
			SUBTOTAL	$	_____
Sales tax (IL addresses only)	8%	×	Subtotal	+	_____
			TOTAL	$	_____

❑ My check or money order is enclosed (payable to Chicago Review Press).

❑ Please bill my Master Card/Visa.

Card Number _____ Exp. _____

Signature _____

Mail order form with payment to **Chicago Review Press**, 814 North Franklin Street, Chicago, IL 60610

To place Master Card/Visa orders by phone, call 1-800-888-4741.

For information regarding quantity discounts contact Chicago Review Press Special Sales Dept., 312-337-0747.